To Harry,

Peace & Joy,

Louis Glaser

YOGA
A PATH TO GOD?

LOUIS HUGHES, OP

MERCIER PRESS

MERCIER PRESS
PO Box 5, 5 French Church Street, Cork
and
16 Hume Street, Dublin 2

Trade enquiries to CMD DISTRIBUTION,
55a Spruce Avenue, Stillorgan Industrial Park, Blackrock, Dublin

© Louis Hughes, OP, 1997

A CIP record for this book is available from the British Library.

ISBN 1 85635 172 6

10   9   8   7   6   5   4   3   2   1

Printed in Ireland by Colour Books Ltd.

CONTENTS

ACKNOWLEDGEMENTS

To Sister Vandana, for insights and many enlightening comments on ashrams; to Noel Molloy, OP, Nagpur; P. Christian Papeians de Morchoven, Saint-Andriesabdij, Bruges and many others for helping me with information on various organisations and individuals studied; to Anne Alcock, for reading the manuscript at each stage and offering many helpful suggestions; to Eamon Maher, for helping me in dealing with material in French.

FOREWORD

During the 1970s I spent six years in India. My official position was as seminary lecturer in philosophy and theology at St Charles' Seminary, Nagpur. However, more personally, this time in India marked for me the start of an enduring involvement with the religious culture of that great land. Since then I have been practising yoga postures and using yogic awareness techniques to prepare for and to facilitate my practice of Christian meditation. While remaining faithful to the Gospel focus, the methods I use are derived from study and personal experimentation with a wide variety of yogic techniques. In this quest I have been greatly inspired and guided by seven individuals who I perceive as pioneers in the dialogue between Christianity and Hinduism. Their lives and work, mainly in the second half of the twentieth century, are the subjects of Part Three of this book. Those who have been inspired by Jean Déchanet, Abhishiktananda, Bede Griffiths, Anthony de Mello, John Main, Amalor and Sister Vandana will see the key role that various forms of yoga played in the way they have lived out their relationship with God.

A related area of research for me, which grew from the first, has been the rise of New Religious Movements (NRMs) – particularly those of Hindu origin. I lecture occasionally and give some specialised guidance in this area. In pursuing my study of NRMs as well as schools of yoga, I have visited ashrams, temples and yoga centres not only in India, but also in Europe and the United States. I have met with leaders and representatives of many movements, and held discussions with those who have practised a wide variety of yogic methods. The impact of these groups – particularly in relation to their ability to focus the energies of their members – cannot be properly appreciated without some understanding of their yogic practice. Part Two of this book covers a small but representative selection of yoga-using groups which are active in western countries today.

What has emerged from some twenty-five years of reading, research, field work and experimentation is an overview of yoga's extension from India to the west. The spiritual values of yoga have travelled with the techniques and pose a challenge both to traditional religious viewpoints and to the prevailing value systems within western society today. This book explores the relationships between yogic practices and religious belief in a range of contexts, both Christian and non-Christian. It attempts to shed light on the question of whether yogic methods can help or hinder an individual's search for meaning and personal growth – specifically whether these methods can facilitate a person's quest for God.

Before moving on to the different yogic movements, some attention will be given to explaining what yoga is. Part One examines the different forms that yoga has taken over the many centuries of its history and then goes on to offer a working definition of yoga. Of necessity a number of Sanskrit terms have had to be used in the text. Generally their meanings are explained as they occur. The exceptions to this are some key terms that are used repeatedly. These are prefixed with an asterisk (*). This means that the term is defined in the Glossary at the back of the book.

DEVELOPMENT AND HISTORY OF YOGA

Yoga may have been practised in India over 4,000 years ago. The evidence for this exists in the form of a soapstone seal found during excavations at the site of the Indus Valley city of Mohenjo-daro. This city was part of an ancient civilisation that flourished in present-day Pakistan before the arrival of Aryan settlers around 2000–1800 BC. The seal found there depicts a horned figured surrounded by a number of animals. The figure is believed to represent *pashupati* or 'Lord of the Beasts', a deity which preceded the Hindu god, *shiva. What is significant in terms of yoga is that the seal's central figure is seated in *bhadrasana*, one of the classic yogic postures for meditation.

It was the Aryans who produced India's earliest religious texts, the *vedas, which date between 1800 and 1000 BC. In two collections of these, known as the *Rigveda* and *Atharvaveda*, there are references to *prana or 'life force'; and *nadis, currents of the life force throughout the body. Specifically, in the *Atharvaveda*, there is a reference to *pranayama or 'breath control' as practised by the mysterious *vratya* brotherhood. Generally speaking, throughout the *vedas there is 'a constant concern with states of consciousness that are far removed from our ordinary awareness'.[1] Techniques for modifying human consciousness are a hallmark of yoga.

A collection of texts known as *upanishads began to emerge soon after the Vedic period from about the eighth to the fourth century BC. Also known as the *vedanta (*veda's end), these express what would become the dominant philosophy and spirituality of Hinduism. What is common to all the *upanishads is the notion of meditation as the chief means to attain transcendental knowledge, although they contain only a few practical instructions on how to meditate. One of the earlier *upanishads, the *Chandogya*, speculates about the syllable AUM, the most fundamental and sacred of all Hindu mantras. In another – the *Taittiriya* – the first use of the word 'yoga' in a technical sense occurs. Later on, the *Katha* *upanishad (fifth century BC) speaks of yoga as 'the steady holding of the senses. Then (the yogi) becomes attentive ...'. The author of the *Shvetashvatara *upanishad* (third century BC) was an adept of sense-withdrawal and meditation. He emphasised an upright posture, control-led breathing and the recitation of the sacred syllable AUM. A century later, the *Maitrayaniya *upanishad* presents yoga as a six-fold path, name-ly: breath-control (*pranayama*), sense-withdrawal (*pratyahara*), medita-tion (*dhyana*), concentration (*dharana*), reflection (*taraka*), and ecstasy (*samadhi*). It also mentions the central channel (*sushumna-*nadi*) that forms the main axis of the body and along which the life-force (*prana*) must be made to rise while reciting AUM.

Yoga or yoga-like processes are to be found in ancient India in reli-gions other than Hinduism. The Jain religion is one of the two serious rivals to Hinduism to have been born on Indian soil. Founded by the as-cetic Mahavira (599–527 BC), Jainism places great emphasis on ethical behaviour as a pre-condition to all yogic or spiritual progress.

Gautama the 'Buddha' or 'Awakened One' (563–483 BC) was the founder of the Buddhist religion and a dedicated yoga practitioner. The seventh stage in his 'noble eightfold path' involves practices such as consciously and passively observing the movements of one's body and in particular the movement of the breath. *Pranayama* or control of the life-force is to be understood in this way within Buddhism and not, as in some Hindu schools of *hatha* yoga, as actively intervening to control or even stop one's breathing. An erect body posture (*asana*) during med-itation is regarded as important.

Karma yoga or 'the yoga of action' is found in its fully developed form in the *Bhagavad-Gita* or 'Song of the Lord'. The *Gita* was written down somewhere between the third century BC and early in the Christ-ian era. It teaches that for action to be wholesome it must have two qualities: objective moral rightness and subjective purity, i.e., it must be performed in a spirit of detachment. However, the essence and heart of yoga is to submit totally to the Supreme Being in the form of Krishna: 'He who is intent on oneness and loves Me, abiding in all beings, in what-ever (state) he exists – that yogin dwells in Me'.[2] Under this aspect of de-voted service to Krishna, the yoga of the *Gita* includes *bhakti* or 'devo-tional' yoga based on love, as well as *karma yoga*.

CLASSICAL YOGA

The yoga of Patanjali as found in his *Yogasutras* (second century AD), is called 'classical' yoga, because he defined systematically the most important elements of yogic theory and practice known up to that time. He did this in order that yoga could stand up to the argumentation made against it by the rival traditions of the time such as *vedanta and Buddhism.

A *sutra* (literally 'thread') is a short pithy statement designed to remind its reader of a much larger body of oral knowledge – and the oral knowledge has now largely disappeared. It is not surprising therefore, that some of Patanjali's *Yogasutras* are obscure or ambiguous. Some of the *sutras* however, are remarkably clear, concise and powerful, as for example, the second one in the first chapter where he defines yoga as 'the restraint of the processes of the mind'.

Patanjali expanded the six-fold path of the *Maitrayaniya* *upanishad to form the *ashtanga* or 'eight-limbed' yogic path – the eight being: restraint *(yama)*, discipline *(niyama)*, posture *(asana)*, breath control *(*prana-yama)*, sense-withdrawal *(pratyahara)*, concentration *(dharana)*, meditation *(dhyana)*, ecstasy *(*samadhi)*.

1. *Restraint:* this involves restraining oneself from such things as greed, violence, lust, stealing, lies and over-indulgence in food and drink.

2. *Discipline:* this calls for positive attitudes and actions in regard to the quest for wisdom, the practice of self-discipline, being content with few material goods and being devoted to *ishvara ('the Lord').

Taken together, restraint and discipline comprise the positive and negative moral requirements, without which any programme of yogic practice is doomed to fail.

3. *Posture:* yogic postures for health was an unknown concept in Patanjali's time. For him posture meant the cultivation of stillness both of body and mind so that real inner work could start. Beginning with the *asanas* and intensifying with each of the stages that follow, the yogi enters into the state of *ekagrata* or 'one-pointedness', a stilling of all bodily and psycho-mental functions that reaches its fulfilment in ecstasy.[3]

4. *Breath control:* techniques of *pranayama lead to deeper relaxation, emotional stability, inner clarity and a growing ability to concentrate.

5. *Sense-withdrawal:* the practices of posture and breath-control them-

selves lead to a de-sensitisation to external stimuli. From this point on the yogi can progressively withdraw his attention from the external world towards some internal object of concentration. Ancient texts use the image of a tortoise contracting its limbs to illustrate this process of withdrawing the five external senses.

6. *Concentration:* the practice of holding one's attention within one's mind on a given point or object such as the image of a deity.

7. *Meditation:* as one spends more and more time in concentration, the object of one's concentration grows to fill the entire space of consciousness. Put in another way, 'a person concentrates more and more upon less and less. The aim is to empty the mind while paradoxically, remaining alert'.[4]

8. *Ecstasy:* the complex of mental and supramental states that are summed up in the word *samadhi* are beyond the power of human language to express. What most seems to define these states is an experience of fusion or non-distinction between the meditator and the object of meditation, accompanied by a mood of bliss.

Patanjali and some later commentators on his *Yogasutras* distinguish at least ten different states of *samadhi* of increasing levels of intensity until finally, the point of no return is reached. Patanjali calls this *kaivalya* or 'aloneness'. The yogi leaves his body and the world of Nature (*prakriti*) and finds perfect bliss in the untarnished experience of the transcendent Self.[5]

Many commentaries have been written on the yoga sutras over the centuries. The most noted commentator was Shankara (788–820), the great proponent of the *advaita* (meaning 'non-dualist') school of *vedanta*. Shankara systematised the insight of the *upanishads* which identified the true inner Self (*atman*) of each individual with ultimate Reality (*brahman*). This one Reality is all that exists. Anything else that can be thought of is merely *maya* ('illusion'). Shankara's philosophy is called *advaita* ('non-dualist').

POST-CLASSICAL YOGA

The centuries following Patanjali are known as the post-classical period. There were many and varied yoga schools extant during this time.

The pashupata tradition began around the second century AD. It venerated *shiva* as 'Lord of the Beasts', the literal meaning of *pashupata* – the beasts in question being unliberated souls. The *pashupatas* were controversial and systematically engaged in anti-social behaviour such as rude gestures and sounds. The resulting public disapproval was designed to enhance their humility and capacity for self-transcendence.

Somewhat more outrageous was the sect of the *kapalikas* or 'skull-bearers', who were certainly in existence by the sixth century. These carried around a human skull for ritual use and also as an eating vessel. They are also believed to have practised black magic and even human sacrifice, as well as sexual practices more commonly associated with later *tantric* schools. To this day small groups of *kapalikas* survive in Assam and Bengal. The *aghori* order arose out of the *kapalika* movement and its members are today both feared and venerated. *Aghoris* use a human skull both as begging bowl and cooking vessel. They live near cremation grounds and eat human flesh from funeral pyres.[6] For them *shiva* is 'lord of the cremation grounds'. In their view a yogi has to be so completely detached and so strongly rooted in meditation that he is not put off by the most distasteful behaviour and surroundings. Through their practices *aghoris* believe that they can become one with *shiva*.

A more socially acceptable development of the post-classical period was the growth of *bhakti* yoga or 'yoga of devotion'. Yogis of this school preach and practise devotion to and service of a personal god as the way to liberation. The god in question is either *shiva* or *vishnu*. Their worshippers are known respectively as Shaivites and Vaishnavas.

The most significant expression of the cult of *shiva* developed in Kashmir around the ninth century. Shaivites hold that *shiva* is the ultimate Reality and pure Being-Consciousness. A branch of Northern Shaivism, known as the *siddha* tradition, was brought to Europe and America by the late Swami Muktananda.[7]

The cult of *vishnu* during this period centred on one or other of his principal *avatars* or incarnations, Rama or Krishna. Krishna, as an *avatar* of *vishnu* became the object of an intensely emotional and at times even erotic spirituality, particularly as expressed in the tenth-century scripture known as the *Bhagavata-Purana* (also known as the *Shrimad-Bhaga-*

vata). This work depicts the God-man Krishna mythologically as husband to 16,108 women, each of whom bore him ten sons and one daughter. Its central theme is *bhakti or devotion towards Krishna. One of the greatest and – from a western point of view – interesting Vaishnavite teacher was Chaitanya (1486–1533), whose name is invoked by the modern Krishna-consciousness movement.[8]

One of the greatest philosophers of the entire *bhakti yoga movement was Ramanuja (1017–1137). His system of thought, known as vishishtha *advaita or 'qualified non-dualism', opposes Shankara's notion that the material world is simply *maya ('illusion'). For Ramanuja liberation does not mean the dissolution of the individual self, but rather the removal of its limitations. It is a kind of fellowship with the Divine Person.

From Patanjali's time to the middle ages a wide variety of relatively short documents known as 'yoga *upanishads' were written. Many of these re-work Patanjali's eightfold path, but some outline additional new approaches to meditation. The *Nada-Bindu *upanishad* describes the practice of the inner sound *(*nada)* which can be located in the right ear during meditation. Focusing on this point can give rise to the experience of sounds such as those produced by the ocean, a waterfall, a kettledrum, a bell or a flute. Through the practice of *nada yoga one can become so completely absorbed in the inner sound that one forgets oneself and in a sense becomes 'identified' with the sound. *Taraka* yoga uses the higher vibrations of both white and coloured light to transcend ordinary consciousness. One technique involves closing the eyes and focusing one's attention on the space between the eyebrows. In this way one may be brought into contact with the unmanifest supreme Light.

The period between the sixth and fourteenth centuries AD was marked particularly by a spirit of experiment and adventure among the yogis of India. The hidden potentials of the human body and the breath, as well as of sound and light were explored in great detail during what is known as the *tantric period.

TANTRIC YOGA
The word *tantra derives from *tan* meaning 'to extend or stretch'. This can be interpreted as 'that which extends understanding'. *Tantric yoga

is mainly a collection of methods aimed at overcoming the duality between ultimate Reality and the conditional human ego. Unlike the highly spiritual and even abstract approach of *advaita *vedanta, tantrism was a grass-roots movement, most of whose followers came from the lower castes and classes of Indian society. It aimed to bring the spiritual quest down to earth, into bodily existence and sexuality. It was this latter especially that gave rise to great hostility in conventional Hindu and Buddhist circles – tantrists were accused of indulging in debauchery under a mantle of spirituality. While these accusations were undoubtedly justified in a number of cases, these were probably the exception rather than the rule.

The tantrists developed a vast range of bodily disciplines and meditative techniques aimed at arousing the *kundalini *shakti or 'serpent power', a psychic energy visualised as coiled at the base of the spine. This *kundalini (serpent) has to be safely conducted along the central *nadi or 'channel' that runs up the centre of the spine. It passes through and awakens in turn each of the seven *cakras or biospiritual 'centres' that lie along the central *nadi. The ultimate aim is to bring the *kundalini up to the *sahasrara *cakra located in the crown of the head. This, it was believed, would lead to a blissful merging of the yogi into the Divine.

There is no unanimity in regard to what precisely all of this means. However, it is possible to relate the *cakras to seven or more areas in the body namely: anus, genital area, solar plexus, heart, throat, between the eyes and crown of the head. These parts of the body are particularly sensitive to stress and psycho-spiritual experience.

The understanding of 'mantra' in *tantric yoga is particularly important. Mantras in the Hindu tradition can be used for three possible purposes: one, to appease the forces of the universe; two, to acquire things magically; and three, to identify with some deity or with Reality itself. For a mantra to be of any benefit, it must be given by a qualified teacher and empowered through a proper initiation ceremony. Mantras can be sung, recited aloud or whispered, repeated mentally or written down. *Japa (recitation) is the word used to describe these practices. It is essential that the practice be done with conscious awareness and not simply by rote.

What a mantra does in the realm of sound, a yantra does for the visual field. The typical yantra is a geometrical diagram composed of a square surround, enclosing a combination of circles, triangles and lotus petal shapes with a *bindu* or 'point' at the centre. The yogi meditates on the yantra and in the higher stages of the practice has to be able to construct it completely in his or her mind. Then she reverses the process and dissolves the yantra bit by bit until eventually it disappears. This dissolution symbolises the yogi's own extinction from the sensible world and assimilation into pure Being-Knowledge-Bliss.

Tantrism is perhaps best known for its ritual of the 'five M's'. These are *madya* (wine), *matsya* (fish), *mamsa* (meat), *mudra* (parched grain) and *maithuna* (sexual intercourse). There are so-called 'right-hand' schools which understand and use these elements in a metaphorical sense, and 'left-hand' schools which use them literally. The object in the latter is not drunkenness, debauchery or (no less reprehensible to the orthodox Hindu) animal slaughter, but altered states of consciousness. Not mentioned among the 'five M's' – although also widely used in *tantric* ceremonies – are narcotic drugs such as cannabis and marijuana.

In *maithuna* or ritual sexual intercourse, the partners embrace not simply as man and woman, but as the god *shiva* and the goddess *shakti*. The act is preceded by hours of painstaking ceremonial preparation. It is performed within a circle of initiates under the direction of the teacher. The requirement is that there be no discharge of semen, since semen is considered a precious product of the life-force and to be conserved at all cost. In *maithuna* as correctly practised, the semen is believed to be transmuted or sublimated into a spiritual substance which nourishes the higher centres in the body and leads to transcendental, rather than sexual, bliss.[9]

HATHA YOGA

Hatha yoga or yoga of the 'force' deals with *prana* or the 'life-force'. It aims at concentrating forcefully all of one's energies in order to attain *samadhi* here and now, in a divinised body. Because *prana* is seen as polarised along the spinal axis, a *hatha* yogi, like a *kundalini* yogi, works at raising the *kundalini*, but with the additional help of certain special techniques:

1. *Purification:* great importance is attached to cleansing the nostrils, sinus passages, throat, stomach, abdomen, bladder and anus by means of air, water, pieces of thread or cloth. This entire discipline of self-purification is sometimes referred to as *kriya* yoga.

2. *Posture:* some of these are intended for prolonged sitting in meditation. Most however are designed for regulating the life-force in the body in order to heal and strengthen it.

3. *Seals and locks:* locks (*bandhas*) involve drawing back the abdomen, contracting the throat or the sphincter muscle with a view to locking the life force into the trunk and thereby stimulating it. Seals (*mudras*) are similar but technically more advanced.

4. *Breath control:* here Patanjali's bare description of **pranayama* as restraining the inhaling and exhaling movements of the breath is fleshed out with a wide repertoire of detailed methods. Diet and clean environment are important for successful practice. There are different kinds of **pranayama* based on different ways of relating the duration of in-breath to out-breath, left and right nostril breathing and the production of various sounds by the breath.

5. *Meditation:* the term *dhyana* ('meditation') is usually understood in *hatha* yoga and tantrism to mean visualisation, typically of one's chosen deity. But in more advanced stages of *dhyana* the attention is simply turned inwards towards the Self (**atman*) in order to be absorbed into it. This is regarded as being the same thing as the union of **shakti* and **shiva* at the crown of the head, giving rise to **samadhi* or complete identification with transcendental Reality.

SUMMARY

The above brief sketch of how yoga has developed over a 5,000 year period gives some idea of the many forms that are found in regard to yogic practices and the philosophies behind the techniques. Most yogis in India have held to a non-dualist philosophy, believing that everything that exists is essentially one, or – to be precise – 'not-two'. Others however, including Patanjali, are dualist and believe in the existence of innumerable separately existing conscious beings. Still others have followed the middle way of Ramanuja in his teaching of a qualified non-dualism. In terms of practices, the differences are even more striking. There are the otherworldly ascetic practices of Vedantic Hindus and Jains. Then there are the *bhakti yogis who express their devotion to a personal god in movement, lively singing and often with great emotion. Altogether different is the strict body-training and asceticism of hatha yoga. Finally, there have been schools of yoga that might be described as controversial, for example the Pashupathas with their deliberately outrageous public behaviour and the more discreet 'left-hand' branch of Tantrism. It is against this background that one has to ask the question: what is yoga?

What is Yoga?

One of the earliest attempts to define yoga is found in the fifth century BC *Katha *upanishad* (VI. 11): 'This they consider to be yoga: the steady holding of the senses. Then the yogin becomes attentive'.[1] Patanjali begins his *Yogasutras* by stating that yoga is 'the restraint of the processes of the mind'.[2] The superficially anarchic *pashupathas* defined yoga as 'the union of the self with the Lord'.[3]

In the *Bhagavad-Gita* Krishna describes yoga as the 'renunciation of the fruit of one's acts'. More generally, the *Gita* understands yoga as a mystical discipline whose goal is the union of the human and divine souls. The *Gita* itself is a small section of the massive *Mahabharata*, a composite epic written and re-edited over many centuries. The *Mahabharata* contains many and often contradictory descriptions of yoga as, for instance, 'method', 'activity', 'force', 'meditation' and 'renunciation'. In general it designates as yoga any practical discipline or activity that leads the soul to *brahman*. In the words of Mircea Eliade: 'If the word "yoga" means many things, that is because yoga is many things. For the epic is the meeting place of countless ascetic and popular traditions, each with its own "yoga" – that is, its particular mystical technique.'[4]

While it may be impossible to give an unambiguous scientific definition of 'yoga', one can arrive at a general description based on the etymology of the Sanskrit term *yoga*. The word *yoga* is derived from the verbal root *yuj* which means 'to join' or 'to connect'. Specifically and more relevant to this enquiry, *yuj* can mean 'to fix one's mind in order to obtain union with the universal spirit'. In the *Bhagavad-Gita* (VI.12) it means 'to meditate'. *Yoga* (derived from *yuj* + a) generally means 'joining', 'union' or 'connection'. In the specifically religious sense it can mean 'meditation', 'union with the universal soul' or 'the practice of devotion, by which union with God is supposed to be obtained'.[5]

Attention needs to be given to the distinction between union as a fact in reality and union as process. There is general agreement among authorities that yoga means processes or methods designed to achieve union with God, rather than a state of union.[6] The processes in question are wide-ranging and operate at the levels of body, senses, mind and spirit. Their rich diversity will be clearly seen when we get to looking at the uses of yoga techniques in differing contemporary contexts.

YOGA AND RELIGION

The term 'yoga' has historically been limited to the Hindu, Buddhist and Jain traditions. However, the basic essence of yoga, which is the process of union or integration, finds expression in all the major world religions. Apart from the many forms of Hindu, Jain and Buddhist yoga, there has also been at least one form of Muslim yoga, though it needs to be emphasised that the word 'yoga' is not used within the Islamic tradition.

The Muslim yoga referred to is the practice of *dhikr*. Eliade comments: 'The similarities between the yogico-tantric technique and the Moslem *dhikr*, or incessant repetition of the name of God, were observed long ago'. This form of prayer is done to the rhythm of one's breath and the posture to be adopted is prescribed in detail: 'squatting on the ground, legs crossed, arms extended round the legs, head bowed between the two knees ...'. There are also references to 'centres' similar to **cakras*.[7]

What about Christianity and yoga? Can there be Christian forms of yoga? Is it legitimate to use the term 'Christian yoga'? The relationship between yoga and Christianity will be looked at in the final section of this book.

Yoga in some New Age and New Religious Movements

The teachers and movements included in this section represent a small fraction of New Age and New Religious Movements which use spiritual practices that can be termed 'yogic'. The reason for selecting these particular groups rather than others is two-fold. They all have a strong presence in western countries today; and between them these groups illustrate virtually all the main forms of yoga.

Before studying the groups individually, a brief look will be taken at the background to the spread of Indian spirituality in the west. Three factors in particular are noteworthy. The first is the Theosophical Society, or 'Theosophy' as it is commonly known. Secondly, from within India itself there is ample evidence of the development of a co-ordinated Hindu missionary strategy aimed at western countries. Finally, the manner in which some New Religions have recruited and held on to their members has on occasion been the subject of controversy.

Theosophy

The Theosophical Society was founded in New York in 1875 by Helena Blavatsky (1833–1893), a Russian medium and Henry Olcott (1832–1907), an American journalist and lawyer. Blavatsky and Olcott claimed to have rediscovered an ancient wisdom that over many centuries and in every part of the world had become obscured by conventional religion. According to this wisdom there exists in the universe not only matter, but also spirit. Spirit is understood to be an invisible energy which can be controlled by those who have discovered or been initiated into its science, namely Theosophy.

From the beginning Theosophy was opposed both to main-line Christianity and scientific dogmatism. It began in time to take a growing interest in the religious philosophies of India and Tibet – its two founders eventually taking up residence in India. The movement enjoyed remarkable growth throughout the last quarter of the nineteenth century and played a key role in the World Parliament of Religions which met in 1893 – of which more in the next section. Today Theosophy has hundreds of branches in the western world and within India. It is included here because it paved the way for the widespread introduction into western countries of yogic practices, and in time facilitated a fully-fledged Hindu missionary outreach.[1]

YOGA GOES WEST

During the nineteenth century a number of Indian gurus visited the west, beginning in 1830 with Ram Mohan Roy, a social reformer and one of the leaders of Indian nationalism. In 1893 Swami Vivekananda (1863–1902), attended the World Parliament of Religions in Chicago. Vivekananda was the leading disciple of Sri Ramakrishna (1836–1886), a Bengali tantrist. Ramakrishna practised, for a time at least, the 'left-handed' *tantric* path, though it is probable that in his later years he confined himself to less literal and less controversial 'right-hand' rituals. Vivekenanda's travelling to the United States and subsequently to Britain and France, led to the establishment of the Vedanta Society, the first successful Hindu mission in the west. Together with the Ramakrishna Math and Mission, of which it is the overseas branch, it continues to practice a variety of 'right-hand' *tantric* yoga rituals.[2]

In the twentieth century Paramahamsa Yogananda (1893–1952) was directed by his guru to bring the practice of yoga to the west. Yogananda settled in Southern California in 1922 and set up the Self Realisation Fellowship, which today has many branches and thousands of members world-wide. Yogananda's teaching, like that of Vivekananda before him, was *advaita-*vedanta*. His now classic book, *Autobiography of a Yogi*, published in 1950, has done much to heighten public awareness of yoga and the traditions that lie behind it. Both Yogananda and preachers of the Vedanta Society attempted to incorporate some Christian teachings into their messages by quoting the words of Jesus in their addresses to westerners – thus enhancing their appeal to the dominant religious ethos of the time.

It was not until after the Second World War that the influence of eastern yogic spiritualities in the west started to become widespread. Hundreds of movements representing between them every technique within the Indian yogic tradition, are now operating outside their Indian homeland. Between them they represent hundreds of thousands of serious practitioners, with probably millions more who have at least dabbled in the practices of one or other. The beliefs as well as the spiritual practices vary from group to group and there can be considerable rivalry. Yet, in regard to the basic thrust of their missionary work in the west they share a common ambition and in the case of most of them, also a common organisation.

HINDUISM'S WORLD MISSION

The *Vishva Hindu Parishad* (VHP) or 'World Hindu Congress' was founded in Bombay in 1964. It is the religious wing of the *Bharatiya Janata* political party (BJP). Both the VHP and the BJP are affiliates of the *Rashtriya Svayamsevak Sangh* (RSS), which was founded in Nagpur in 1925 in order to produce the leaders for a renascent Hindu India. Among the objectives of the VHP as listed in its Constitution are 'to establish an order of missionaries, both lay and ordained, for the purpose of propagating dynamic Hinduism'and 'to open seminaries for training such missionaries to diffuse the spiritual and ethical principles of Hinduism throughout the world for the welfare of humanity as a whole.'[3] While the use of Christian religious terms like 'missionary' and 'seminary' is striking, there is here no pretence at incorporating Gospel language or values. Apart from its multitude of Indian operations, the VHP has established itself in many other countries. There are 36 branches in the United States.

Within India the *Vishva Hindu Parishad* organises major conferences on Hinduism that attract tens of thousands of participants. Its journal *Hindu Vishva* makes specific mention of many guru associations that co-operate with the VHP. These include the Ramakrishna Mission and Vedanta Societies, Yogananda's Self-Realisation Fellowship, the Hare Krishnas, Sai Baba, the Sivananda Ashram and its various off-shoots in the west, the Iyengar Yoga Association and Transcendental Meditation.[4] Tibetan Buddhism is also involved, since the Dalai Lama presided over the VHP Conference of 1979. Another fundamentalist Hindu publication, *Hinduism Today* noted the activities of movements such as Radha-soami and the Brahma Kumaris in its January 1991 issue. It stated: 'A small army of yoga missionaries – hatha, raja, siddha and kundalini – beautifully trained in the last ten years, is about to set upon the western world. They may not call themselves Hindu, but Hindus know where yoga comes from and where it goes'.[5]

The VHP's mission goes well beyond religious worship and spirituality. The organisation is best known, particularly outside India, for its involvement in a riot that led to the demolition of the 500-year old Babri Masjid mosque at Ayodhya on 6 December 1992. It attempted to justify this action by claiming that the mosque had been built by Muslim invaders on the site of an ancient temple marking the spot where the god Ram had been born thousands of years ago. In reality, earlier archaeological investigations of the Babri Masjid area had produced no evidence of any pre-existing Hindu temple.[6] For its part in the destruction of the Babri Masjid and in subsequent rioting which led to the deaths of several thousand people, the VHP was banned for two years by the Indian government. This ban was re-imposed in January 1995, but seems to have had little effect on the organisation's activities.[7]

The VHP differs from earlier Hindu missionary organisations in that it has a political agenda to impose order and uniformity on Hindu society. It claims to speak and act on behalf of all of India's 800,000,000 Hindus. This claim is rejected not only by secular Hindus but also by the majority of Hinduism's spiritual leaders. The most pretigious of these are the four hereditary successors of the philosopher-monk Shankara, who are known as Shankaracharyas. These preside over four monasteries founded by Shankara himself early in the ninth century – one for each point of the compass. Three of the Shankaracharyas oppose the VHP. The one who supports it – the Shankaracharya of Jyotirmath in the Himalayas – is in a relatively weak position, since his seat as the Shankaracharya of the north is also claimed by a rival, based at Dwaraka in Gujarat. It is evident that the VHP does not enjoy nearly as much support from India's Hindu community as it claims.[8]

THE ISSUE OF 'MIND CONTROL'
Some of the groups studied in this book have been the subject of considerable hostility and in the popular mind have been labelled 'cults'.

The term 'anti-cult movement' has been used to describe those who oppose certain New Religious Movements on psychological or psychiatric grounds. The members of the 'anti-cult movement' are for the most part ex-members and families of those who have joined one group or other. They accuse the 'cults' of systematic deception, engendering fear and the use of exploitative mind controlling techniques to recruit and hold on to their members.[9]

'Cults' may derive their teachings from Hinduism, Buddhism, Islam, Christianity or any of the world's religions. Some use elements from more than one religious tradition. Others might be termed 'New Age' or 'Neo-Pagan'. Still others are not religious at all in any conventional sense of the word. Those studied in this section almost all have their origins within the Hindu tradition.

The issues raised by the 'anti-cult movement' are most serious. However, it is not within the scope of the present work to give them the detailed study that they deserve. What can be said however, is that the approach to New Religious Movements taken by the 'anti-cult movement' tends to equate them all somewhat indiscriminately. By stressing almost exclusively the negative psychological features it sees them as having in common, it ignores the rich diversity that exists between different groups. The chapters that follow will attempt to show how each of the groups studied – whether those deemed by some to be 'cults' or not – is profoundly shaped by its own particular yogic practices. Attention will be drawn to some instances of connections between the uses of particular forms of yoga and subsequent damage – potential and actual – to those who practise them.

TONY QUINN'S POPULAR YOGA

Most people in western countries first encounter yoga as a system of physical exercises or as a way to relax. Typical aims include coping with stress and high blood pressure, health, strength and a good-looking body. Richard Hittleman, through his many books and television programmes which reached hundreds of thousands particularly in the United States, pioneered the 'yoga for health' movement from the 1950s onwards. In the decades that followed many schools of popular yoga have sprung up in every part of the western world. This chapter looks at a representative and highly successful movement in Ireland.

Dubliner Tony Quinn claims that he introduced yoga to Ireland in 1971. Although a small number of people had been practising yoga exercises in the preceding decades, Quinn's claim is valid if one is talking about the systematic organising and publicising of courses in yoga on a nation-wide basis. Currently he presides over a high-profile corporation that handles not only courses and teacher training in yoga, but similar programmes for Ki (or Chi) massage, holistic medicine and other varied self-help therapies including one called 'body sculpting'. Since 1983 he has been publishing a quarterly newspaper *Blueprint for Living* which is delivered free on a door-to-door basis to over 500,000 homes. Tony Quinn yoga classes are run at any one time in no less than thirty different centres throughout the country. He also owns a chain of stores marketing products ranging from health-foods to nature-based cosmetics and vitamin tablets.

By any standard Tony Quinn's has to be among the great 'success stories' in terms of bringing yogic methods to the attention and into the lives of ordinary people. He attributes this success to his own personal philosophy which he occasionally calls 'The Tony Quinn System'. His approach and philosophy are typical of a vast number of yoga groups throughout Europe, North America and other western countries. As such it will now be looked at in some detail.

THE TONY QUINN SYSTEM OF PHILOSOPHY

From the pages of *Blueprint for Living* the essentials of Tony Quinn's system can be put into place. According to him there is one ultimate principle underlying every human being and the entire universe. This reality he refers to variously as the 'Self', 'Life' or 'Energy': '... inside each of us is a life source from which emanates life in the form of energy ... We refer to it as the Self. Equally then, we can say that the purpose of my system is self-expression or self-realisation.' And he sees this 'Self' or 'Life' as being 'our true nature'. Moreover, this 'Life' is not some abstract or remote philosophical entity, but is alive and active and can be experienced directly by each individual person within himself or herself: 'Yes, you can actually feel what is sometimes referred to as life-force. With this comes a delightful discovery – the happiness, even to euphoria, that comes when life is being freely expressed within you'. 'Life' or the 'Self' is seen as a benign force that always tends to act in our best interests: 'The Self takes care of us and keeps us in perfect health'.[1]

According to Quinn, the 'very purpose of human life' is 'to give birth to the Self'.[2] And the way this can happen is simplicity itself: 'all we have to do is be still. Anybody who has the courage to put what is being said to the test can become aware for themselves of their true nature, Life/Self'. It is not a question of anything that people have to do in order that they can have life – rather it is simply a matter of 'almost relaxing into life and allowing it to flow through them unhindered'.[3]

Allowing Life to flow or the Self to be born is believed to open the door to all kinds of improvements in a person's life. The most spectacular benefits are likely to be in the area of health. Most illnesses are – Quinn believes – caused by people not allowing the life energies of nature to flow through them: 'It seemed that the struggles and strivings of the patient somehow impeded or blocked the flow of curative power'. However, on the other hand, 'when we stop struggling, what we want is done for us ...'[4] Relaxing and letting go is Quinn's key to health. In working with those who come to him for healing, the first thing he does is 'relax all effort on the part of the patient – mainly mental (stress, tension, worries, problems, complexes, etc.). This allows their self-healing force, life force, self-normalising energy to work unhindered and allows the real person to emerge.' And this process is not simply about elimi-

29

nating disease. It also involves a comprehensive improvement in the person's quality of life. He continues: 'Not only can that bring about a cure but to me what is the most important aspect of all is that it can lift the person up to new levels of self and life-improvement, health, healing and success never before experienced'.[5]

Tony Quinn's therapy can take more active forms that can be used by anybody to bring about an improvement in another person's life: 'hold thoughts of healing or life improvement or job improvement for the person and just allow life to flow through you to them, unhindered'.[6] This method can be employed even to gain something as mundane as money: 'It's merely enough to hold the successful outcome in your mind. For example, say you wanted a sum of money – you would merely then in that non-resistant state hold the idea of the sum of money and it would come about'.[7] The benefits of this method can be extended to a person who is not present at the time: 'I maintain that it is possible to sit on your own in a room and if you take a picture or letter from a person that you have never met and then let life flow from you unhindered to that person then you will obtain benefit'.[8] In dealing with a therapist a person need simply 'write down clearly what he or she wants out of life, hand the request to the therapist to work on for them, and relax'.[9] The above philosophy has been developed on a large scale within the Tony Quinn organisation. Each issue of *Blueprint for Living* carries a section entitled 'Postal Requests' in which remedies for illnesses ranging from panic attacks and anxiety to strokes and cancer, as well as examination results, lottery winnings and improved relationships are reported by grateful readers. These – the paper tells us – were the results of 'the Tony Quinn system of prayer and positive thinking for a successful outcome'.[10]

UNCONSCIOUS ATTENTION

In recent years Quinn has begun interviewing well-known sports people in *Blueprint for Living*, so that his readers can be inspired and learn from them. Niall Quinn, Irish international soccer striker, learnt the advantages of positive thinking while recovering from a knee injury that had kept him out of the game for six months. He believes that this has helped him not just to recover fully, but to become 20% fitter than he had been before being injured: 'if you can believe that things are happening in your body, believe in your strength, then you can be 20% or 25% better ...'[11] Boxer Steve Collins engaged Tony Quinn as a 'mental coach' in the build-up to his successful world title fight with Chris Eubank in 1995. As he puts it: 'Tony worked with me to get this certainty into the very deepest part of my mind'.[12] This didn't only help him to win a world title. He claims that during the fight it also enabled him to control pain, fatigue and even bleeding. As a result he believes that his body had fully recovered from the effects of the fight within forty-five minutes instead of the usual two to three weeks.

At the core of Quinn's approach to situations like the above is what he calls 'unconscious attention'. This differs from the more usual conscious attention that people have of an object in that it requires no effort of will, no decision to hold one's awareness to the object. Unconscious attention is 'where you are focused, so absorbed with what is taking place that your entire attention is taken up by it and no part of you is left over to be consciously aware that you are paying attention'.[13] In this way, Quinn holds, a sportsperson or anyone else can effortlessly keep images of a positive outcome before their mind and so emerge with greater success.

In his most dramatic demonstration of the technique of unconscious attention, Tony Quinn has helped four patients undergo surgery without anaesthetic. The results as reported seem extraordinary. Not only were the patients free from pain – they seemed to have enjoyed their operations! Typical comments were: 'From the moment it began an amazing feeling of well-being and relaxation came over me'; 'It was just a beautiful feeling, because you really felt so complete'; 'It was a bit disappointing when the operation was over. At that point I was in a state of very deep relaxation and I just didn't want to come out of it'. These views were endorsed by the four doctors involved.[14]

POSITIVE THINKING AND CHRISTIAN PRAYER

The combination of 'prayer' with positive thinking is a feature of Tony Quinn's system, which *Blueprint for Living* frequently alludes to. In fact he seems to identify positive thinking with prayer: 'If this (*healing, life improvement, job improvement)* seems strange to you, maybe it won't if we sum it up in one word – Prayer'.[15] He speaks about how he arrived at this insight: 'I came to a part in the Gospels where Jesus said: "If you want something, believe that you have it, without any inner doubt, and I give you my word that it will come about ..." I felt here was a formula for living given to us by Jesus Himself ... A formula for successful living, that is the only formula known beyond doubt to have worked miracles and to be guaranteed by Jesus. I was fascinated and decided there and then that that would be my formula for living'.[16] He uses the word 'FAITH' (and in capital letters) to describe this attitude of mind and heart. This invocation of Gospel authority to support his system needs to be looked at closely.

The statement attributed to Jesus in the above passage is not found in any one of the four Gospels. At best it is a very rough paraphrase of the words of Jesus and seems to be derived either from Matthew 21.22 ('If you believe, you will receive whatever you ask for in prayer') or particularly Mark 11.24 ('When you pray and ask for something, believe that you have received it, and you will be given whatever you ask for').

In a more recent issue of *Blueprint* Quinn specifically referred to the above text from Mark and to other Gospel texts in support of his philosophy. Here too he speaks of how as a boy 'he developed a passionate interest in reading the Gospels'. To his young mind Jesus was 'the greatest real live magician of all'. He goes on to speak of how certain passages revealed the philosophy upon which he was to base his life. He quotes Matthew 9.29, Mark 9.23, Mark 11.23 and again Mark 11.24.[17] All speak of the powerful efficacy of 'faith' or 'belief' (depending how the particular English translation renders the Greek *pistis* or *pisteuein)*. However, it is Mark 11.24 that most closely resembles Quinn's oft-quoted 'formula' for living. As such its meaning will now be examined, but in the context of the entire passage in which it occurs, Mark 11.22–25: 'Have faith in God. I assure you that whoever tells this hill to get up and throw itself in the sea and does not doubt in his heart, but believes that what he says will happen, it will be done for him. For this reason I tell you: When you pray and ask for something, believe that you have received it, and you will be given whatever you ask for. And when you stand and pray, forgive anything you may have against anyone, so that your Father in heaven will forgive the wrongs you have done'.[18]

Can this passage be used to support Tony Quinn's philosophy of positive thinking? In particular, is Quinn's understanding and use of the word 'belief' the same as the Gospel meaning of 'belief'? A typical Christian commentary on this part of the Gospel of Mark states: 'We cannot expect to receive literally "whatever" we ask, however selfish and contrary to God's will. Perhaps verse 25 was added to guard against such a notion'.[19] This is the verse that speaks about forgiveness of others as a requisite for prayer. More significant is that, unlike Tony Quinn, the Gospels always use the terms 'faith' and 'asking' in the context of prayer to a personal God in whom one believes – hence the exhortation of Jesus – 'Have faith in God' with which the passage quoted begins. Christian prayer is always in relation to God who is Other than oneself. And one might add that it is only when there are distinct persons, that inter-personal love and any form of relating become possible. When one asks for something in prayer, one is calling on God as Creator or Redeemer, and always with a sense of dependence and trust. Prayer in general is fundamentally about surrender to rather than control of another. One seeks to 'let go' to a Higher Being because in faith one trusts that He/She has the wisdom and power to know and do what is best for each person. Thus when one 'asks in prayer' one speaks in a spirit of humility and vulnerability – in the belief that God knows best and cares most for each person and ultimately has the last word.

The Tony Quinn System operates from a contrary perspective. The highest principle that it recognises – 'Life', 'Energy' or 'Self' – is there simply to be used by each person to advance his or her own agenda. This principle is quite appropriately referred to in *Blueprint for Living* as 'it', since it is quite impersonal. It is not any kind of Supreme Being that we have to serve. Instead, it serves us and is even part of us, 'our true nature'.[20] Thus, in the Quinn philosophy, the centre of the universe is the individual person himself/herself and not God or even any form of Higher Power. This is a very different world-view from that of Jesus, who frequently 'spent the entire night in prayer to God'. Consequently, to quote Jesus as supporting the Tony Quinn System is to misunderstand the Gospel.

33

Tony Quinn's 'unconscious attention' is not a recent discovery. Ernest Wood (1883–1965) belonged to the earlier generation of western scholars who studied yoga and helped open up the practice to non-Indians. He wrote extensively about the last three stages of Patanjali's yoga – concentration, meditation and ecstasy (though Wood preferred the term 'contemplation' instead of 'ecstasy' as the English equivalent of *samadhi).* In explaining the relationship between the three, he states that they form a connected series. At the earlier part of the series 'there is an act of will in which you tell your mind to keep to that subject and not to wander away from it'. After a certain amount of practice, focusing one's attention can become easier and even habitual: 'the act of concentration is still there while the meditation is going on, though it has been forgotten – "subconscious" or "unconscious" is the new word for this ...'; '... one forgets oneself, is taken out of oneself, yet is intensely conscious'. What is implied here is that one is both conscious and unconscious at the same time – conscious of the object upon which attention is focused, and unconscious of this same consciousness. And this, Wood tells us, is 'the chief characteristic of ecstasy or rapture', which he associates with *samadhi* as understood by Patanjali. It will be evident from the above that the psychological state which Quinn terms 'unconscious attention' has for centuries been part of the classical yoga tradition.[21]

A more significant connection between Quinn's philosophy and Indian religion is to be found in the fundamental principle upon which his system is based – Self, Life or Energy. Quinn acknowledges that this principle is very ancient: 'In fact that life-essence, that energy, was written about thousands of years ago ...'[22] The identification of the Self (with a capital 'S') as being the true nature of the human person links Quinn's philosophy to the Vedantic school within Hinduism. There too the true nature of the person is 'self' (*atman),* and this self is identified completely with *brahman,* the Creator God. But Quinn's concept of the 'the Self' seems less subtle than the Vedantic *atman,* in that the *atman* cannot be directly perceived, or even imagined: 'it is an abstraction, an essence tied to the thought – or more properly, the mystical vision – that there is a base or ground or substratum to the universe that is beyond words to describe ...'[23] In contrast to this, Quinn states simply that 'the inner self, the real person, is manifested without effort when body and mind are fully relaxed'.[24]

Quinn says that '... the purpose of my system is self-expression or self-realisation'.[25] Here it is worth noting that the term 'self-realisation' has a specific meaning in the contexts of eastern religions, expressed for example in the name 'Self-Realisation Fellowship' of the neo-Vedantic yoga movement established by Paramahamsa Yogananda (1893–1952). The 'self' in question here is very much more than one's self in the every-day meaning of the term. Within the Vedantic tradition Self-Realisation means mystically experiencing one's true identity as being not different from *atman, the Self and *brahma, the Supreme Being.[26] The term used to describe this mystical state is *advaita ('non-duality').

CONCLUSION

The front page of many editions of Blueprint for Living carries a small frame entitled 'For First Time Readers'. A statement in the frame says that the paper is 'unique among newspapers because it brings people only good news'. And it is certainly true that Tony Quinn's paper con-trasts sharply with conventional dailies that today more than ever seem to bring an endless series of stories of war, violence, horrific accidents, economic crises, corruption in high places – in short all the messiness of human life on this planet. In the media generally the dark side of exis-tence is high-lighted and at times exaggerated in the extreme. It is there-fore, hardly surprising that so many people have taken to Tony Quinn's version of good news in which only that which is positive, pleasant, gentle and life-giving finds a place. His programme of yoga is designed to enlarge this positive picture. Blueprint for Living abounds in pho-tographs of beautiful, well-tanned bodies, letters from satisfied clients and articles inviting one to take a course in yoga, holistic healing or stress management. There are advertisements for vitamin tablets and products for restoring original hair colour or banishing foot and body odour. One full page article advocates a course in yoga postures with the slogan 'Get in shape for Summer'. Since 1994 Quinn has renamed his paper Blueprint for Successful Living.

This glowing picture of modern living stands in sharp contrast to the viewpoint of traditional Hindu yoga where the emphasis is on escaping from this earthly life which it sees only as a form of bondage.

If traditional Indian yoga can in general be described as 'otherworldly', then Tony Quinn's yoga is most definitely 'this worldly'. Objectives such as business success, weight loss and having thicker hair would sound very strange in a traditional Indian yoga centre. A second point of contrast is that whereas Quinn will report 'only good news' in his paper, for the Hindu and Buddhist traditions, this world is a vale of sorrow – 'bad news' in fact.

Tony Quinn has adapted a variety of techniques from the Indian yogic tradition, for example: postures, breathing and a rather simplified version of Vedantic philosophy – together with other practices of vaguely eastern origin such as massage and methods of alternative healing. However, the Tony Quinn philosophy is essentially a belief in the power of Positive Thinking. As such it is more a product of the west than of the east and can take its place alongside so many other movements within the contemporary New Age culture.

CLASSICAL HATHA YOGAS

The groups examined in this chapter represent the transplanting of classical yogic traditions from India to North America and Europe. The leaders of the various schools are Indians who are highly regarded by their co-nationals. They are mainly concerned with the use of traditional *hatha* yoga techniques such as postures, breathing, diet and meditation to achieve Self-realisation or the *advaitic* experience as taught in the *upanishads* and by Shankara. Temple-worship – particularly of *shiva* – is part of the daily round in their ashrams within India and quite often in western countries too. The *Yogasutras* of Patanjali is a fundamental text for reflection and practice.

The western branches of these organisations frequently offer courses with a distinctly 'New Age' flavour in such areas as positive thinking, yoga for health and healing therapies such as aromatherapy and massage. In addition some groups offer scientific demonstrations of the physiological power of yoga techniques. A significant departure from Hindu tradition is their active canvassing for new followers – particularly among spiritually hungry westerners.

From the many traditional *hatha* yoga teachers and schools operating in North America and Europe, just a few outstanding examples are included here.

SIVANANDA YOGA VEDANTA

The Sivananda Yoga Vedanta Centre in San Francisco is part of a successful international yoga movement founded in 1959 by Swami Visnu Devananda, a disciple of the late Swami Sivananda of Rishikesh. Its rooms are liberally decorated with pictures of the Hindu god Krishna, together with Vishnu Devananda and Swami Sivananda, Devananda's teacher. Most people make their initial acquaintance with the centre through one of the monthly open days, when the centre invites the interested public to come, free of charge, for a day of yogic postures, breathing exercises, chanting, meditation and discussion. From there many will go on to participate in the various courses and weekends that are available, not just on yoga, but on vegetarian cooking, natural healing, and performances of Indian music and dance.

Swami Vishnu Devananda has simplified the *ashtanga or 'eight-limbed' yoga of Patanjali into five basic principles which he believes are particularly adapted to the needs of modern women and men. These principles are: relaxation, breathing, exercise, diet and right thinking. In the San Francisco Centre yogic postures and breathing are taught and practised with the correctness that one would expect to find in an Indian yogic centre. The diet is strictly vegetarian. For Vishnu Devananda, right thinking means Vedantic philosophy, the heart of which is to know by experience the 'oneness of all existence'.[1]

A feature of the San Francisco Centre is its meditation room. This has an ornate altar table decorated with flowers, oil lamp, incense-holders and images of figures ranging from Ganesha, the Elephant-god, to Swami Sivananda. The garlanded pictures of deities that surround the altar include one of Jesus. What members of the ashram refer to as 'yoga church' takes place here. This consists of meditation and chanting sessions, sometimes accompanied by a sermon. All-night vigils are occasionally held in the meditation room.

Vishnu Devananda (born 1927) became a disciple of Swami Sivananda in 1947 and trained under him at his Rishikesh ashram, becoming one of his most accomplished pupils. He came to the west in 1957 at Sivananda's direction and has since been based in Canada. He has founded ashrams and yoga centres throughout North America and Europe and has trained several thousand yoga teachers. An indication of the scale of his influence can be had from the fact that one of his books, *The Complete Illustrated Book of Yoga*, has sold over a million copies.

SIVANANDA ASHRAM, RISHIKESH

Vishnu Devananda's teacher, Swami Sivananda (1887–1963), was a doctor from south India who spent a number of years practising in Malaya. In 1923 he renounced the world and began to live the life of a *sannyasi* (ascetic) in a dilapidated, scorpion-infested hut beside the river Ganges above Rishikesh. He also started a small charitable dispensary in 1927, a service which was greatly appreciated in the area round about. In time however, people started coming to him more for spiritual guidance than for medical care. This in turn led him in 1932 to establish a small ashram in an abandoned cowshed. The ashram attracted growing numbers of pilgrims during the remainder of Sivananda's life and after his death in 1963. Sivananda ashram today is one of the finest in Rishikesh. It consists of a large complex of temples, halls, dining and residential units.

Primarily because of his prolific writing Sivananda's influence extends far beyond Rishikesh. The Divine Life Society, which he founded in 1937 to promote spiritual, medical, social and publishing activities, now has over 300 branches world-wide. He has left behind him a number of outstanding disciples. Swami Chidananda (born 1916) succeeded Sivananda as president of the society after the latter's death in 1963. To him is due the credit for the organisation's rapid spread in the west. However, effective leadership is now in the hands of Swami Krishnananda (born 1921).[2]

The visitor to Sivananda ashram will be impressed by the ashram's contemplative spirit, peaceful atmosphere and warm hospitality. The daily programme encompasses the full sweep of traditional yogic living: training in postures and breathing techniques, group chanting and meditation, temple worship and lectures on the Hindu scriptures. Members and most visitors to the ashram express their submission to the authority of the *acharyaguru* (presiding swami) by means of the *panchanga pranam* or 'five-part salutation'. This involves simultaneously touching one's knee's, elbows and forehead to the ground in front of the swami. Its significance is that one accepts the guru's word and authority as coming directly from God. This perception of the guru as divine is based on what for millenia has been implicit in some (though contradicted by other) *upanishadic* texts. Thus, for example, the Brihadaranyaka *upanishad* (I, iv, 10): 'Who so thus knows that he is Brahman, becomes this whole (universe). Even the gods have not the power to cause him to un-Be, for he becomes their own self'.[3] Texts like this were used by Shankara to develop the *advaita* philosophy in the middle ages. However, it is only with the advent of modern Indian guruism that the ideology of the 'God-man' guru is fully asserted.[4] In the words of Swami Sivananda: 'Guru is Brahman himself. Guru is Ishwara. Guru is God'.[5]

SATYANANDA SARASWATI AND THE BIHAR SCHOOL

Swami Satyananda Saraswati was born in 1923 at Almorah in the foot-hills of the Himalayas. At the age of nineteen, while still living at home, he was initiated into *tantra by Sukhman Giri, a female yogi from Nepal. Thus he was already well versed in the language of *cakras, *nadis and *kundalini before he joined the Sivananda ashram in Rishikesh in 1943. Having spent twelve years with Swami Sivananda he left Rishikesh and became a wandering ascetic. In 1962 he founded the International Yoga Fellowship Movement, establishing its headquarters at Munger in the state of Bihar – hence the term 'Bihar School', often used in reference to Satyananda's movement. Since 1968 he has gone on many internation-al lecture tours and has run yoga teacher training courses for Europeans. The Bihar school was one of the first to train female and foreign *san-nyasis on a large scale.

Satyananda continued Sivananda's broad approach which integ-rated a wide variety of yogic techniques with charitable works and so-cial development. He has in addition given a particular emphasis to *tantra including, it is said, the 'left-hand' path.[6] He has also pioneered the practice of *yoga nidra* or 'yogic sleep', a form of deep relaxation med-itation. Based on ancient and little known *tantric practices, *yoga nidra* involves placing one's awareness on different parts of the body in turn and in this way putting each of them 'to sleep'. As taught by Satyanan-da these exercises are frequently accompanied by guided imagery prac-tices that seem to have more to do with modern psychotherapy than traditional *tantra. He has used *yoga nidra* as a tool for stress control, coping with high blood pressure and as cancer therapy. Psychological applications include speed learning and coping with addictions.[7]

In 1983, in order to give more attention to his own spiritual practice, Satyananda handed over the administration of the Bihar school to his disciple Niranjanananda. Between 1989 and 1994, in the company of a senior female disciple, Satyananda undertook a five year period of in-tense meditation and austerity to 'stabilise the pattern of his sadhana and spiritual life'.[8] During this time he practised a daily ritual called the *panch agni vrat* or 'rite of the five fires' which involves sitting surround-ed by four fires – the fifth 'fire' being the sun's heat overhead – in order to obtain purification.

Swami Rama

Swami Rama was born in 1925 into a North Indian Brahmin family. He was, however, raised by a Bengali yogi and in 1949 became a monk in the Shankaracharya order. This position he relinquished in 1952 in order to further his own teaching goals. His academic background includes the study of medicine and philosophy at various universities including Oxford.

In 1970 in a project sponsored by the Menninger Foundation in the United States, he gave a demonstration of conscious control of autonomic bodily functions. He prevented his heart from pumping blood for seventeen seconds and created a brain wave pattern normally found only in deep sleep, while remaining fully aware of his environment.[9] In describing his work he says: 'my purpose is to create a bridge between the east and west, by establishing a centre of learning from where I can faithfully deliver the message of the sages of the east'.[10] In order to carry out this mission he established the Himalayan Institute in rural Pennsylvania in 1971. The iInstitute offers programmes in meditation, yoga techniques and related therapies.

Iyengar's Dynamic Yoga

B. K. S. Iyengar was born in 1918 into a priestly Hindu family. At the age of sixteen he started practising yoga exercises as a remedy for illness. The results were so satisfactory that he decided to dedicate his life to the teaching of yogic postures and breathing. He became known in the west as a result of his contact with the violinist Yehudi Menuhin, who had sought his help with a back problem which was threatening his musical career. Iyengar went on to develop a world-wide network of yoga centres devoted to the spread of his own distinctive method of teaching. He himself is based at his institute in Pune in India, which he runs together with his son and daughter, both highly regarded teachers in their own right.

Like most hatha yoga teachers, the philosophy followed by Iyengar is based on the eight limbs of the Patanjali yoga. According to Iyengar, adhering to even one of these yogic principles leads to inner peace and harmony. His method of teaching the yogic postures is renowned for its detailed correctness. It is also physically demanding. The student, while holding a posture for a considerable length of time, is required to flex and tauten various groups of muscles. This is intended in time to bring the student to 'the apex of yoga by practising physical, mental and spiritual techniques in the hardest postures and breathing exercises'.[11] It is hardly surprising therefore, that Iyengar defines hatha yoga as 'the way towards realisation through rigorous discipline'.[12] This definition is implemented with gusto in all posture classes run according to the Iyengar method.

Within the Iyengar system, control of the body, the breath, senses and mind are seen as steps on the way to becoming *a yukta* – one who is in communion with God' or with the Universal Spirit.[13] Iyengar broadens the philosophy of Patanjali to take in elements of *vedanta* and even Christianity. On numerous occasions he uses expressions that remind one of the Gospels. An example of this is his reference to the path of sensual satisfaction being a broad one which is followed by many but which leads to destruction, whereas the path of yoga is 'narrow and difficult to tread, and there are few who find it'.[14] The role of *ishvara* or a personal God is stressed somewhat more than in the original Patanjali tradition: God dwells within the individual and is the person's Inner Self. He is the one who 'shapes and controls the universe'. The yogi is called to dedicate all his actions to the Lord. Iyengar's is a 'no nonsense' God who expects his devotees to give of their all from the beginning. Then 'after one has exhausted one's own resources and still not succeeded, one turns to the Lord for help ...'[15]

BHAKTI YOGA AND THE HARE KRISHNAS

The vast majority of religious Hindus do not practise yogic postures, controlled breathing or sophisticated meditation techniques. What is, however, virtually universal is the practice *japa or the devout repetition of God's name, aloud or in silence. When this recitation is done systematically and with heart-felt, even passionate devotion to God, one is practising *bhakti yoga or 'yoga of devotion'. In the west, the best-known group which practises *bhakti yoga is the International Society for Krishna Consciousness.

The International Society for Krishna Consciousness was founded in 1966 by a seventy year-old Indian Swami, Bhaktivedanta Prabhupada. He had left India and arrived in New York penniless less than twelve months previously. Prabhupada was born Abhay Charan De in 1896 in Calcutta, India. His family were devout members of the *Gaudiya Vaisnava* sect, a group that worships Krishna in the tradition of Mahaprabhu Chaitanya (1485–1533). Chaitanya taught that *bhakti was the only way to spiritual liberation. He understood *bhakti as the 'affectionate service of God for his sake alone' or 'to love God as one's lover'.[1]

Abhay's religious background was significant for the future of the religious movement he was to start. Of particular importance was his meeting in 1922 with Bhaktisiddhanta Sarasvati Thakura, spiritual head of the *Gaudiya Math,* a monastery-temple and centre for Chaitanya's followers in Calcutta. Bhaktisiddhanta was in fact the latest of a series of disciples stretching back to Chaitanya himself. He and his predecessor, Bhaktivinoda Thakura had taught that the teachings of Chaitanya were intended not just for a particular sect or nation, but for all the people of the world. From their first meeting in the Math, Bhaktisiddhanta urged young Abhay to take up the mission of spreading Chaitanya's message of devotion to Krishna throughout the world. Initially Abhay was reluctant, preferring to continue giving his energy to Gandhi's campaign of passive resistance to British rule in India. Abhay's spiritual development was gradual. It was not until 1932, when he and his wife and family were living in Allahabad, that he took initiation and formally became Bhaktisiddhanta's disciple.

Following Bhaktisiddhanta's death in 1936 and against the background of India's war-time difficulties and Independence struggle, Abhay took a more active role in the mission of the Gaudiya Vaisnavas. In 1944 he started a magazine which he called *Back to Godhead*. He was convinced that the answer to all the world's difficulties was to be found in the study of the *Bhagavad-Gita* and other scriptures and in particular in the repetitive chanting of the *mahamantra* (literally 'great mantra') This is the mantra with which westerners were to become familiar decades later through the public chanting of the Hare Krishnas.

Abhay's profession of pharmaceutical salesman involved travel and in the early days he was able to combine this with the work of distributing his magazine. Eventually however, with the intensification of his preaching and writing about Krishna, his family life suffered. His wife did not share his intense religious interest, so he left home permanently, basing himself first in Delhi and later in Vrindaban, eighty miles to the south. For the Gaudiya Vaisnavas Vrindaban is a holy place, believed to be the place where Krishna lived as the incarnation of the god *vishnu some five thousand years ago. There in 1959 Abhay formally renounced the world by being initiated into the state of *sannyasa or 'renunciation' of the world. From that time on he was to be known as Bhaktivedanta Swami. It was only years later that his American followers honoured him with the name Prabhupada which means the one 'at whose feet masters sit'.[2]

Bhaktivedanta had already retired from his professional work at the time of his *sannyasa. He now began to concentrate more than ever on his writing. In addition to regular issues of *Back to Godhead*, he undertook his own commentary on the tenth century devotional work, *Shrimad Bhagavatam*, one of the most sacred of scriptures for worshippers of Krishna. By the time of his departure for the United States, he had published the first three of fifty volumes, each of more than 400 pages.

Prabhupada arrived virtually penniless in New York in September 1965, having only the names of a few people who might offer him hospitality. By February 1966 he had his own tiny rented room in Manhattan, in which he offered three lectures weekly and continued working on the *Shrimad Bhagavatam*. A few young people, mainly from the 1960s 'counter-culture' started coming to see him, often out of curiosity that an elderly Indian swami should be living in a rundown area of New York. He spoke to them and introduced them to mantra chanting. This in turn drew more followers and the 'Hare Krishna' movement – named after the chant – began to spread. Within a few months the International Society for Krishna Consciousness (ISKCON) was born.

The price Prabhupada paid for the establishment of his movement was disimproved health. He returned to India in 1967. Though he did make a number of foreign trips thereafter, from 1970 onwards Vrindaban was the base from which he continued to build up the Krishna Consciousness movement. At the time of his death on November 14, 1977, ISKCON had grown into an international organisation with more than 100 ashrams, schools, temples, institutes and farm communities mainly in North America, Europe and India. Its membership included more than 4,000 whom Prabhupada had personally initiated and a total following, which it was claimed, numbered several millions. Probably the best-known of these was one of the 'Beatles', George Harrison, who donated his country estate outside London to the movement. He also gave his musical talents to publicising Krishna Consciousness. In 1969 George and a group of devotees produced a hit single, 'The Hare Krishna Mantra' which reached number 12 in the charts.[3]

HARE KRISHNA PHILOSOPHY
Members of ISKCON – called 'devotees' – are required to live a strict life. Rising each morning at around 4am, they take a cold shower and immediately enter into a programme of chanting, prayers, scripture lessons and offerings to the gods before having breakfast around 7.30. Much of the day is spent chanting in the streets, handing out literature or other work. The evening is usually given over to meditation, spiritual reading and more chanting. Devotees are strict vegetarians. Alcohol, tobacco, tea and coffee are out and though some members marry, all must observe a very strict code of sexual behaviour.

The Hare Krishnas, along with Hindus generally, believe in reincarnation. One can observe, for example, that as the human body ages and changes, the individual remains the same. They conclude from this that when the body dies, the spirit-soul, unless it qualifies to 'go back home, back to Godhead', continues in the world by taking on another body. This new body can be any one of the '8,400,000 bodily forms' of plants, insects, fish, birds, beasts – as well as human beings – which are found in the world.[4] The particular outcome is determined by the manner in which one has lived the life just ended.

For members of ISKCON the supreme scriptural authority is the *vedas and other spiritual writings of ancient India. They believe that the *vedas were not written in historical time, but have existed from the beginning of creation. In fact Vedic literature as a whole is considered by ISKCON to be a kind of instruction manual which was given to humankind together with the world, in order that people might understand how to live in and use the world correctly.[5] Prabhupada and ISKCON hold for a literal understanding of the Hindu scriptures.

The single most revered text for Krishna devotees is the Bhagavad-Gita, which is a small section within the massive Mahabharata epic. The Gita exemplifies the guiding and consoling presence of Krishna in human affairs, specifically in the moral anguish of Prince Arjuna prior to and during the great battle of Kurukshetra. Unlike Prabhupada modern indologists interpret the Mahabharata symbolically and regard Kurukshetra as a mythological rather than a historical event. These scholars generally assign a date to the Bhagavad-Gita either a little before or a little after the time of Christ. In contrast, the Hare Krishnas hold that the Gita 'is said to date back 5,000 years to the time when Krishna incarnated on earth to teach this sacred message'.[6] Hare Krishnas and Hindus generally, revere the Gita as a sacred text, and accord it a status not unlike that held by the Gospels for Christians. Daily meditation on selected portions of the Gita and of Prabhupada's massive commentary on it, is expected of all members of ISKCON. It is believed that this practice keeps a person spiritually in tune with God and helps one to become more whole-hearted in serving Krishna. Humankind's greatest need is the practice of *bhakti or loving devotion to Krishna. The Bhagavad-Gita teaches that *bhakti yoga is the highest form of yoga. It quotes Krishna as saying: 'of all yogas, he who always abides in Me with great faith, worshipping Me in transcendental loving service, is most intimately united with Me in yoga and is the highest of all' (B.-G. 6.47).[7]

Chaitanya identified Krishna with *vishnu and the Absolute or Supreme Being.[8] Chaitanya's followers, including members of ISKCON, believe that Krishna is God himself and not merely one of his incarnations. But they go further than this. They regard Chaitanya as much more than a teacher and source of inspiration. For them he is an *avatar or incarnation of Krishna disguised as his own devotee. As such there can be 'no higher principle of truth than Chaitanya-Krishna' who is 'the supreme ultimate principle'.[9] Hence the title Mahaprabhu or 'Great Lord' by which they address Chaitanya.

Does ISKCON regard Mahaprabhu Chaitanya as the founder of the Krishna consciousness movement? Prabhupada says: '... actually the original founder of this movement is Lord Krishna himself, since it was founded a very long time ago, but is coming down to human society by disciplic succession'.[10] 'Disciplic succession' is frequently referred to in Prabhupada's writings. He insists that those who would become Krishna conscious must enter into a relationship of unquestioning obedience to a human swami or teacher. In this regard the Hare Krisha movement is no different from many other traditional Indian guru movements.

SANKIRTANA AND THE MAHAMANTRA

*Sankirtana or 'group singing' as practised by members of ISKCON, is very similar to what Chaitanya and his followers practised in the villages of Bengal in the early sixteenth century. It involves loud chanting of the names of Krishna and Rama, usually to the accompaniment of drums, cymbals and other instruments. It is an emotionally charged exercise and participants usually break into spontaneous dancing or jumping movements. Prabhupada and the Hare Krishnas consider Mahaprabhu Chaitanya to be the originator of *sankirtana.[11] However, it was almost certainly practised long before his time.[12] *Sankirtana is an age-old and highly effective *bhakti yoga technique. Like energetic devotional singing within other religious traditions including Christianity, it releases tension and can greatly help to focus awareness on the object of veneration.

Prabhupada made extraordinary claims about the power of chanting the name of Krishna and Rama in the mahamantra. He saw it as much more than a method of prayer or meditation. The *mahamantra* is the vehicle whereby one is set free from the slavery of material nature and brought to a spiritual stage of super-consciousness or Krishna-consciousness.[13] It cleanses the heart and brings about self-realisation or God-realisation. It is the panacea for every social and human evil. If enough people practise it, it will lead infallibly to world peace. Death and suffering will lose their terrors once it is realised that man's real nature is spiritual, and profound and lasting happiness will result.[14] To explain why this particular form of chanting God's names is so powerful, Prabhupada said that it is because 'this transcendental sound vibration is non-different from Him'.[15]

The benefits of the *mahamantra* are believed to result not just when it is performed as *sankirtana* or in group singing, but also when it is recited individually and quietly by all Krishna devotees. The *japa* beads which each one carries around with him in a cloth bag has 108 beads and is used rather like the Catholic rosary to count the *mahamantras* in private recitation. Each member of ISKCON is required at the very least to do sixteen rounds of the beads daily – that is in addition to group singing in public or before temple idols.

For ISKCON the practice of *sankirtana* is a powerful instrument of evangelisation. Very many of those who join the Hare Krishnas first encounter the movement through its public singing of the *mahamantra*. For some, the experience of *sankirtana*, both on the street and indoors, is overwhelming. One observer who hesitated to join in the singing in the street, later went on to embrace Krishna consciousness. He reported: 'I saw the devotees chanting, and those magic words, magic words, "Hare Krishna, Hare Krishna, Krishna Krishna, Hare Hare/Hare Rama, Hare Rama, Rama Rama, Hare Hare!" So I finally gave in and joined them, repeating over and over again. It certainly felt good afterwards. Two days later I went to *kirtana* at the devotee's private house. This time it hit me! I was lost in bliss, divine bliss! ... I was overwhelmed! Now Krishna Consciousness really had a hold on me, and I can't believe it's all happened so fast!'[16]

Hindus and orientals in general agree that sound itself has creative power and that the recitation of certain sacred words and names puts one in contact with or even makes present what or who the mantra signifies.[17] The heart is believed to be purified and one's life centred on the deity who is the object of the mantra.[18] However, these spiritual effects come about only if one's mantra recitation is accompanied by meditation on the meaning of the mantra.[19] With practice the element of meditation will tend to predominate and the recitation become quieter, more interior and eventually perhaps cease altogether. *Sankirtana according to the Hare Krishnas is quite different from this. One does not have to understand the meaning of the *mahamantra*, nor is any special effort at concentration necessary. One simply chants and the beneficial results come about automatically and directly from the particular set of sound vibrations produced in the chanting.[20] All this is possible because – it is claimed – the *mahamantra* functions on a 'spiritual platform' and therefore 'surpasses all lower strata of consciousness – namely sensual, mental and intellectual'.[21]

CHANTING AND HEALTH

What Prabhupada called the 'lower strata'of the emotions, senses and the entire body are very much involved in ISKCON's congregational celebrations. Prabhupada lists some of their more extreme manifestations: '(1) being stopped as though dumb, (2) perspiration, (3) standing up of hairs on the body, (4) dislocation of voice, (5) trembling, (6) fading of the body, (7) crying in ecstasy and (8) trance'.[22]

Chaitanya himself practised *sankirtana in a very intense form. He danced and sang of the love of Krishna and his consort Radha, he fell into trances. His *sankirtana developed from small groups into public processions and led to a Vaishnava revivalist movement. Singing from door to door Chaitanya and his followers would call on people to lead holy lives. On visiting the famous temple at Puri, Chaitanya danced and swooned before the idols.[23] The question of the psychological soundness of this practice was raised long before the International Society of Krishna Consciousness was established. During his lifetime there were those who questioned Chaitanya's sanity.[24] The distinguished historian of Indian philosophy, S. N. Dasgupta, writing in the 1940s stated: 'The religious life of Chaitanya unfolds unique pathological symptoms of devotion which are perhaps unparalleled in the history of any other

saints that we know of ... His intoxication and his love for Krishna gradually so increased that he developed symptoms almost of madness and
epilepsy. Blood came out of the pores of his hair, his teeth chattered, his
body shrank in a moment and at the next appeared to swell up ...
Without the life of Chaitanya our storehouse of pathological religious
experience would have been wanting in one of the most fruitful har-
vests of pure emotionalism in religion'.[25]

A former member of ISKCON described the long-term effects that
membership and in particular chanting had on the mental health of
some devotees. Whereas most devotees would spend about two hours
a day chanting their rounds to Krishna, a number would require four or
five hours to get through them: 'There's not a whole lot of work to do
around the temple, so we would just let them chant all day. Eventually
these people deteriorated to the point where they couldn't get their
chanting done. They would become slower, and we couldn't get them
to work or do anything. They were basket cases'.[26] Research on the effects of prolonged chanting within ISKCON as well as corresponding
practices within some other religious groupings point to a phenomenon
that investigators Flo Conway and Jim Siegelman have termed 'information disease'.

Conway and Siegelman completed a survey in 1981 of 400 former
members from 48 different new religious groups.[27] In it they tabulated
the psychological effects of membership on former members. These included 'floating' in and out of altered states of consciousness, night-
mares, amnesia and inability to break rhythms of chanting. The Hare
Krishnas were found to have higher instances of all of the above than
occurred in former members of the Unification Church, the Divine
Light Mission, The Way International and the Church of Scientology.
The authors also detected a correlation between the severity of these effects and the numbers of hours spent each week on ritual and indoctri-
nation. Here the Krishnas, at around 70 hours weekly, were well ahead
of the others. The research of Conway and Siegelman points to some
link between excessively prolonged chanting of the *mahamantra* –
whether in group *sankirtana* or as individual practice – and psychological disturbance.

Prior to his death Prabhupada had appointed a 22-man Governing Body Commission (GBC) to administer ISKCON. At the core of the GBC were eleven 'initiating gurus' authorised to initiate new members in different regions of the world. Since then the Hare Krishnas have rarely been out of the spotlight of controversy. Six of Prabhupada's chosen eleven have had to relinquish their posts – some of them in spectacular circumstances.

James Immel or Jayatirthadas had responsibility for over-seeing the development of Krishna Consciousness in Britain, Ireland and South Africa. In April 1982 he was expelled from ISKCON because of persistent addiction to the drug LSD and also because of sexual indiscretions.[28] Following his expulsion, Immel changed his name to Tirthapada and founded a breakaway group which he called the 'Peace Krishnas'. This group was characterised by particularly ecstatic group chanting sessions. In 1987 he was hacked to death in London by one of his most devoted but mentally unstable followers, who was upset at the news that the guru he had identified with Krishna had deserted his wife for another woman.

Keith Ham aka Kirtananda, with Prabhupada's backing had established a large rural commune in West Virginia called New Vrindaban. It included a luxuriously constructed temple named Prabhupada's Palace of Gold. The problems at New Vrindaban included the murders in 1983 of a commune member, Chuck St Denis and in 1986 of Steve Bryant, a former devotee turned critic of Kirtananda. At a meeting of the Governing Body Committee at Mayapur, India in 1987 Kirtananda was expelled from ISKCON.[29] Since that date, he has continued to run the New Vrindaban community as an independent branch of the Krishna-consciousness movement. Entitled the International Society for Krishna Consciousness of West Virginia, its members on occasion wear brown monk-like habits in place of Indian-style dress.[30]

Hansadutta or Hans Kary, another of the eleven 'initiating' gurus appointed by Prabhupada before his death, parted company with ISKCON in 1984. He set up a small independent Krishna Consciousness community near San Francisco entitled the Nam Hatta World Sankirtan Party.[31]

In the wake of intense theological and organisational debate with-in ISKCON, some members sought guidance from Prabhupada's 'god-brother', Bhakti Rakshak Sridhara Maharaj (1895–1988). By 'god-broth-er' is meant that both had been initiated by the same guru, Bhaktisid-dhanta. These moves have so far led to the establishment of two further independent Krishna Consciousness movements with branches in the west: the Sri Chaitanya Mandal based in San Jose, California and the Gaudiya Vaishnava Society with headquarters in San Francisco. These groups are at one with ISKCON in beliefs and practice. The Krishna Con-sciousness movement generally is now smaller and leaner. It appears to have entered a more mature and stable phase in its development and al-so one that is less dogged by controversy.[32]

CONCLUSION

Sri Bhaktivedanta Swami Prabhupada was an impressive representa-tive of the contemporary wave of evangelical Hindus who saw it as their mission to spread their religious faith and values in western coun-tries. As long as he was personally able to supervise the spread of the movement, it remained broadly faithful to his form of *bhakti yoga or 'devotional union' with Krishna. In keeping with the fundamentalist tradition of which he was part, Prabhupada interpreted the Vaishnava Scriptures – especially the battle passages in the Mahabharata and Bhagavad-Gita – literally. For instance, upon hearing reports of attacks on New Vrindaban in 1973, he is reported to have written to Kirtanan-da: 'why are you not keeping guns? Where violence is, there must be vi-olence. We are not followers of Gandhi's philosophy. Ours began on the field of war'.[33] In saying this he may have been unwittingly preparing the way for the stock-piling of weapons that would later prove so dis-astrous for the movement.

The devotional practices of the *bhakti yoga tradition are highly re-garded by large numbers of Indian Hindus. The technique of energetic emotional group singing and dancing are psychologically powerful. A parallel western example of these practices is to be found within the Pentecostal or Charismatic movement. As an instrument of spiritual growth these practices do presuppose authentic and competent spiritual guidance. When properly supervised, *sankirtana* like its western Christian counterparts, allows for the 'unfreezing' of a disciple's personality and for the putting in place of a new spiritually and a morally reformed persona.

Where leadership is deficient, the power of *bhakti* yoga techniques may allow the very opposite to take place. Many of ISKCON's American disciples – particularly the earliest recruits who rose rapidly through the movement's ranks – were drawn from the hippie culture of the 1960s and were drug addicted when they joined. Prabhupada's ill-health necessitated his departure from the scene in July 1967, less than two years after his arrival in the United States. There had been too little time for him to adequately form the movement's American leadership and thus the stage was set for the subsequent decline in ISKCON's fortunes. The rise and decline of the Hare Krishnas is a graphic illustration of what can go wrong when a powerful spiritual practice – in this case *bhakti* yoga, the 'yoga of devotion' – is transplanted into a context where ethical training cannot keep pace with spiritual and mystical aspiration.

Mantra Yoga and TM

This chapter looks at movements in which some elements of t
al Hinduism are present but not evident to the external obser
School of Economic Science, also known as the School of Phi
runs courses in philosophy and economics. The ads do not state ____ __
philosophy in question is *vedanta*, and that what one is being invited to
embrace is in reality not academic learning but initiation into a tightly-
knit religious group and a form of meditation which uses the name of
the Hindu god Ram as its mantra.

The school was founded in the 1930s by Andrew McLaren
(1883–1975), a British left-wing politician. It was only when his son Leon
(b. 1911) took control of the school in 1947 that its focus shifted from
economics to philosophy and religion. Here, the earlier and still potent
influences are the esoteric teachings of George Gurdjieff (1877–1949)
and Pyotr Ouspensky (1878–1948). Equally significant however, are
Leon McLaren's regular meetings in India since the early 1960s with the
Shankaracharya of Jyotirmath in the Himalayas, one of four official in-
heritors of the Vedantic teaching of Shankara. The school has followed
the teaching of this guru's successor ever since. This Indian connection
has an interesting background. McLaren had worked closely with Maharishi Mahesh Yogi in the early 1960s and in fact at one time encouraged
members of the school to be initiated into TM. It was the Maharishi who
introduced McLaren to the Shankaracharya – Swami Brahmananda
Saraswati, who was the Maharishi's own guru. Although McLaren and
the Maharishi fell out later in the 1960s, an initiation ritual and meditation as practised by the school today remain remarkably similar to TM,
the main subject of this chapter.[1]

Transcendental Meditation was developed by Maharishi Mahesh
Yogi, who was born Mahesh Prasad Varma in Central India in 1911 (or
1918 according to some sources). Having graduated in physics from
Allahabad University in 1940, he studied for thirteen years at Jyotirmath in the Himalayas with Swami Brahmananda Saraswati (1869–1953),
usually referred to by his title 'Guru Dev'. Guru Dev had discovered (or
possibly rediscovered) from Hindu Scriptures a simple yoga meditation

technique. It is said that just before he died, he commissioned Mahesh Yogi to make this form of meditation widely known. The result is what is now known as Transcendental Meditation or TM. In 1956 Varma took to himself the title *maharishi* which means 'great seer'. The Maharishi brought his technique to the United States and other countries in 1959. In the same year he founded the International Meditation Society. During the next few years the practice of TM spread rapidly, helped in no small way by the involvement of a number of celebrities such as the Beatles and actresses Mia Farrow and Jane Fonda.

Over the following decades the Maharishi initiated a number of additional projects. He founded the Maharishi International University (MIU) at Fairfield, Iowa in 1971. MIU offers undergraduate and postgraduate courses in the Maharishi's philosophy. In 1972 he launched his World Plan which aimed at establishing 3,600 meditation centres throughout the world, each staffed with a thousand TM teachers. He predicted that his plan would lead to a significant improvement in the psychological, social and political condition of the world. In 1976 he created the World Government of the Age of Enlightenment, described as non-political but holding authority in the domain of consciousness. It claims to be able to solve the problems of all governments. More recently the Natural Law party was formed in 1992 to give expression to the Maharishi's political ideas. It has enjoyed very little electoral success. All of the afore-mentioned organisations are administered by the World Plan Executive Council, which though officially unconnected with the Maharishi, is nonetheless dominated by his ideas.

Transcendental Meditation is presented by its promoters as a 'simple natural technique which allows mental activity to settle down to a state of increasing inner quietness, producing deep mental and physical rest'.[2] It is taught only by an approved TM teacher for a fee which is roughly based on what a would-be meditator earns in a week. The teaching consists of an introductory session, an hour-long personal initiation ceremony and three shorter follow-up consultations. During initiation the candidate is given a mantra which is not to be revealed to anyone. Thereafter the practice of TM involves the silent repetition of the mantra twice daily for at least twenty minutes.[3]

The promoters of Transcendental Meditation claim that its regular practice produces beneficial results of at least four kinds: physiological, psychological, spiritual and socio-political. Each of these areas will now be looked at in turn.

1. *Physiological:* TM's promoters say that it is the ideal method for coping with physical stress. Its practice has physiological effects which were scientifically measured in an important study by Wallace and Benson published in 1972.[4] During meditation, oxygen consumption, carbon dioxide elimination, cardiac output, heart rate, and respiratory rate decrease significantly. There is an increase in Galvanic Skin Resistance, i.e., the electrical resistance of the skin to a small electric current. Electroencephalogram patterns or 'brain-waves' reveal an intensification of slow 'alpha' (and sometimes also 'theta') activity. All of these observations are symptomatic of a 'slowing down' of the metabolism that is more radical than that produced in sleep or under hypnosis.

Systematic studies like the above do indeed support the claim that practising TM quickly leads to a deep state of physical relaxation. However, some of these studies also suggest that other forms of meditation produce the same results. Dr Herbert Benson has already been mentioned in connection with some of the early research into the benefits of TM, much of which was sponsored by the organisation itself. In his bestselling paperback, *The Relaxation Response*, published in 1975, Benson distanced himself a little from his earlier studies. By 'relaxation response' he means the nervous system's natural ability to rid itself effortlessly of stress and produce the symptoms mentioned in the preceding paragraph. According to Benson 'there is not a single method that is unique in eliciting the Relaxation Response. For example, Transcendental Meditation is one of the many techniques that incorporate these components. However, we believe that it is not necessary to use the specific method and specific secret, personal sound taught by Transcendental Meditation'.[5] Benson refers to research results which indicate that the same technique that TM uses allied to any sound or phrase or prayer or mantra, brings about the same physiological results. Among alternate techniques known to produce the Relaxation Response in a similar way to TM, are zen and yoga.[6] This is hardly surprising in regard to yoga particularly, since the techniques used in TM have their origins in the Indian yogic tradition.

2. *Psychological:* At the level of mind it is claimed that transcendental meditation leads to increased learning ability and other personal benefits such as acceptance of self and others, personal integration and self-identity. TM 'develops creative intelligence and improves clarity of perception at all levels of experience'.[7] Improvements of the mental kind are by their nature difficult to establish. While supporters of TM are enthusiastic in advancing such claims, some ex-meditators have gone so far as to take the Maharishi International University to court for failing to deliver on promised results for which they had paid thousands of dollars. Instead of 'improved memory, reduced stress, perfect health, increased academic ability and expanded awareness' they claimed that they ended up with 'misery, beset by anxiety, irritability, rage, guilt and loss of memory'.[8]

Some serious research supports the view that TM can produce adverse psychological effects such as anxiety, physical and mental tension and boredom. Contrary to what one group of researchers expected, these negative results were most marked among TM teachers and others who had been meditating for eighteen months and longer. 'These data suggest that the longer a person stays in TM and the more committed a person becomes to TM as a way of life ... the greater the likelihood he or she will experience adverse effects'.[9]

3. *Spiritual:* The Maharishi speaks about various states of consciousness that the individual experiences as he progresses in TM. These include 'transcendental consciousness', 'cosmic consciousness' and 'God consciousness'. These states are not clearly distinguishable one from another and tend to overlap. Together they involve the mind's transcending or going beyond itself. As he puts it: 'The mind loses its individuality and becomes cosmic mind ... Here the mind does not exist, it becomes existence'.[10] This statement approximates to one of the key doctrines of Vedantic Hinduism which is the Maharishi's religious background. This teaching, rooted in the *upanishads*, speaks of a mystical state – *advaita* – in which the individual personal self is experienced as being not different from the universal Self or Spirit (*atman*) which is identical with *brahman* or ultimate reality.

This self-transcendence which is the objective of TM is described in the movement's literature as a 'fourth state' of consciousness that is distinct from and superior to the other 'three physiologically defined states – wakefulness, dreaming and deep sleep'.[11] This alternative way of looking at the experience of self-transcendence also has a long history. The notion of four progressive levels of consciousness, beginning at the waking state, is well known within the philosophical traditions of India as far back as the *upanishads. The third of these states – that of dreamless or deep sleep – is regarded as mystically significant. In contrast to the dream state there is a cessation of imaginative awareness in dreamless sleep. 'The embodied self is then said to attain a temporary union with the Absolute'.[12] The state of dreamless sleep is however far surpassed by the state known as *turiya* (derived from *chaturiya* meaning 'fourth'). This state can be testified to only by highly gifted yogis. In the *turiya* state 'the self fully reveals itself'.[13] The *turiya* state is the goal of the spiritual quest within the Vedantic yoga tradition.

4. *Social:* According to the TM organisation significant social benefits result from the practice of Transcendental Meditation in concentrated groups of a certain size. Consumption of narcotic drugs and crime generally are said to be significantly reduced. In fact, if a certain minimum proportion of a country's population can be persuaded to take up TM, it is supposed to lead to a dramatic reduction in crime and anti-social behaviour. This outcome is promised by the 'Maharishi technology of the unified field', a supposedly scientific theory which attempts to apply the language of physics to human consciousness: '... only the square root of one percent of the population of the country (a slightly larger proportion for a country with a small population) practising the Maharishi Technology of the Unified Field in any one place in the country is sufficient to fully awaken national consciousness.' As a result 'law and order are spontaneously maintained, and administration becomes simple, effective, free from problems, and free from the elements of fear and punishment'.[14]

The social and political benefits which are supposed to have followed the practice of TM on a large-scale, have been extensively publicised by the World Plan Executive Council for over two decades. National governments in every continent have been lobbied to adopt the technology as part of their programme. Despite the alleged benefits in the areas of education, health, agriculture, economics and security, there have been few takers. Nevertheless, TM has not been without its backers in official quarters, particularly in the United States.

The view that TM offers only positive and universally acceptable benefits in the educational, social and mental health areas received its most spectacular endorsement in a resolution passed in 1972 in the Illinois House of Representatives, encouraging the state's Department of Mental Health 'to incorporate the course in TM in the drug abuse programs' of the state. This resolution also encouraged all education institutions to 'study the feasibility of courses in Transcendental Meditation ... on their campuses.'[15] The introduction of TM instruction into American public education was to have far-reaching consequences for the Transcendental Meditation organisation, as will be seen shortly.

IS TRANSCENDENTAL MEDITATION A RELIGION?
The connection between Transcendental Meditation and the yogic tradition is expressly acknowledged by the movement itself: 'Yoga means "union" – the union of the ordinary self with the large Self. And this is what transcendental meditation is all about. So we can say that transcendental meditation is the heart and soul of yoga.' In addition the organisation states that TM 'has profound relevance to religion'. However, the organisation has always strenuously denied that it is itself a religion. Rather, TM is 'a purely practical technique, which can be practised by anyone, whatever his beliefs or lack of beliefs'.[16] This opinion however, has not been universally accepted.

In October 1977 the United States District Court in Newark, New Jersey ruled that the use of taxpayers' money to teach Transcendental Meditation and its theoretical counterpart the Science of Creative Intelligence (SCI) in New Jersey public schools was a violation of the First Amendment to the United States Constitution, on the grounds that TM is religious by nature.[17] This judgement was upheld in the United States Court of Appeal in Philadelphia in February 1978. The case had been initiated by the Spiritual Counterfeits Project, an evangelical group based in Berkeley, California. The transcript of the case highlights the key factors which led the court to its conclusion that TM is in fact a religion, rather than a science or simply a practical technique. These were: 1) The initiation ceremony, whereby the aspiring Transcendental Meditator is introduced to the practice; and 2) The TM mantra.

THE TM MANTRA
Every TM beginner without exception is given a mantra or word to be repeated mentally every time he or she sits down to meditate. The mantra is given in the course of the initiation ceremony. The aspiring meditator is told that this is her or his own personal mantra and that it must on no account be revealed to anyone else – otherwise it will lose its power.

The sense of specialness in which the giving of the TM mantra is shrouded might seem to suggest to the individual meditator that he or she alone has been given that mantra and that the TM organisation must have dispensed many thousands, even millions of different mantras to corresponding numbers of meditators. The reality, as told by instructors who have defected from the movement over the years, is rather different. A variety of sources suggest that only sixteen different mantras are given to new meditators. Moreover, the mantra one gets is determined solely by one's age at the time of initiation. The complete list seems to be as follows:[18]

Age	Mantra	Age	Mantra
0 – 11	*Eng*	26 – 29	*Shiring*
12 – 13	*Em*	30 – 34	*Shirim*
14 – 15	*Enga*	35 – 39	*Hiring*
16 – 17	*Ema*	40 – 44	*Hirim*
18 – 19	*Ieng*	45 – 49	*Kiring*
20 – 21	*Iem*	50 – 54	*Kirim*
22 – 23	*Ienga*	55 – 59	*Sham*
24 – 25	*Iema*	60 +	*Shama*

It will readily be seen that the mantras listed above can be grouped into pairs whose spelling and pronunciation differ only very slightly from one another, i.e., depending on whether the consonant 'm' or the more nasal 'ng' is used, or on whether one includes or omits an 'a' sound after the mantra's final consonant. These differences arise only in translation and result from different ways of pronouncing or writing in English the same Sanskrit sound.[19] The eight English words in the left-hand column are derived in these ways from no more than two Sanskrit words: those on the right from four. Thus in reality the sixteen different TM mantras are sixteen anglicised versions of just six Sanskrit mantras.

More significantly, these mantras, far from being sounds without meaning as is sometimes thought, have in fact a long history of use in the context of Hindu worship and meditation. Most, if not all, of them are regarded as *bija* or 'seed' mantras and, according to one contemporary authority on yoga – Swami Vishnu Devananda – should be handled with special care: '*Bija* Mantras and certain mystic Mantras ... should not be repeated by those who are not well acquainted with them and with the Sanskrit language'.[20] Vishnu Devananda gives a breakdown on a number of *bija* Mantras. For example, if one takes the TM mantras *Kiring* and *Kirim* together as one mantra (which Vishnu Devananda renders as *Kreem*): 'With this mantra Kalika should be worshipped. *Ka* is Kali, *ra* is Brahman, and *ee* is Mahamaya.' Likewise *Hiring* and *Hirim* (alternately *Hreem*): 'This is the mantra of Mahamaya or Bhuvaneshvari. *Ha* means Siva, *ra* is prakriti, *ee* means Mahamaya.' *Shiring* and *Shirim* (alternately *Shreem*) are used in the worship of the goddess of wealth, Lakshmi, while *Ieng, Iem, Ienga* and *Iema* (alternately *Aim*) is the mantra of the goddess Saraswati.[21] Agehananda Bharati, a leading authority on *tantric yoga, states that the *bija* mantras *Aim* and *Hreem* are used to invoke the goddess *shakti* in the course of *tantric ritual sex.[22]

For Hindus and Buddhists generally mantras are much more than words. Particularly within the *tantric yoga tradition a mantra is regarded as 'a vehicle of salvation'.[23] The peculiar power that mantras have is due to the fact that 'they *are* – or at least, if correctly recited, *can become* – the "objects" they represent. Each god, for example, and each degree of sanctity have a *bija-mantra*, a "mystical sound", which is their "seed", their "support" – that is, their very being'.[24] However, it has always been believed in the east that mantras, if they are to be effective, cannot simply be picked up and used haphazardly. An initiation by a qualified guru who imparts the mantra is required. This too is the background to the TM initiation ceremony.

THE INITIATION CEREMONY

Every person without exception who wants to learn TM is required to go through an initiation ceremony in Sanskrit with his or her teacher. The would-be meditator is asked to bring along a white handkerchief, some fruit and flowers. These 'gifts' are placed on a small table in front of a picture of Brahmananda Saraswati, who in the course of the ritual is addressed with his honorary title 'Guru Dev'. Among the extracts from the ritual text which were quoted in English by the presiding judge of the Appeal Court was:

> Guru in the glory of Brahma,
> Guru in the glory of Vishnu,
> Guru in the glory of the great Lord Shiva,
> Guru in the glory of the personified transcendental
>   fulness of Brahman, to Him,
> to Shri Guru Dev adorned with glory,
> I bow down.[25]

The text is never translated for the initiates. In the context of the symbolic gifts which the initiate brings to the ceremony, it was concluded by the courts and by other authorities that 'the "initiation", at which the pupil is present, includes, on the one hand, ritual offering with an invocation to Hindu gods in Sanskrit; on the other, the use of a mantra of the name of a Hindu god, in the actual process of meditation itself'.[26]

The notion and practice of *diksha* or 'initiation' is common to Hinduism and Buddhism. A guru or teacher is even defined as 'one who gives *diksha*' to others who are ready to receive it.[27] The competent guru will be able to recognise when a person is ready for a particular rite, and also what kind of meditation, etc., is likely to yield the best results for each aspirant.[28]

Offerings of fruit and flowers have for centuries been an integral part of *tantric yoga rituals. The flowers offered by the aspirant are used in that part of the ceremony known as *pushpanjali* or 'flower offering'. Other gifts may also be given, which in modern times can include a cheque.[29] However, the heart of every initiation ceremony is the giving of a mantra. During the ritual the guru whispers the aspirant's special mantra into his/her ear, having first warned him to keep it secret and not to write it down.[30]

It will be clear from the above accounts of mantra and initiation just how deeply rooted Transcendental Meditation is in the classical traditions of Hindu yoga. An examination of how TM is organised and practised within India itself will serve to further underline this point.

TM IN INDIA

In 1980 the Maharishi moved himself and the centre of power of the entire TM movement from the United States back to India. There he presides over two different kinds of activity. One of these caters for the Maharishi's foreign disciples and was for a time located in a prominent office building in downtown Delhi. A larger development located at Noida near Delhi is the specially constructed township of Maharishi Nagar. Here there is an ashram community of several thousand Indians including large numbers of boys aged from 10 years up who are on a 12 year educational programme in Vedic science. The main building at Noida is a large temple, in which the ashram members worship before images of the elephant-headed god Ganesh, the goddess Parvati and the Maharishi's teacher Guru Dev. The centrepiece of the altar is however, a picture of the Maharishi himself. The Maharishi's plans for Noida include 'Vedaland', a mythological theme park along the lines of Disneyland, but designed to impart spiritual enlightenment to its visitors.

TM's third main Indian centre of activity is Shankaracharya Nagar, the movement's oldest ashram on the banks of the Ganges in the holy city of Rishikesh. The Maharishi himself has expressly forbidden all foreigners from entering this ashram and this order is enforced by guards at the gate. Thus, the Maharishi appears to be practising *de facto* apartheid in India. The group of westerners in the heart of the nation's capital serve to promote the notion of TM as being 'non-religious', while at Noida and Rishikesh the profoundly Hindu character of Transcendental Meditation is evidenced.[31]

THE FUTURE OF TM

The Transcendental Meditation movement reached a peak in 1975 when a total of over 292,000 new members were initiated in the United

States. This was also the year when the Maharishi's photograph graced the cover of *Time* magazine. Since that year the numbers of new members has been on the decline. In particular from 1977 (the year of that crucial New Jersey court decision) onwards United States initiations have been running at less than 1,000 per month.[32] As the numbers taking up the practice of the basic meditation decreases, greater emphasis has been put on the more advanced and esoteric *siddhi* programme, basic training in which costs more than £1,000. The *siddhi* programme is designed to produce some of the more spectacular results which (it is claimed) meditation can produce, for example, levitation or 'yogic flying'. By these terms the organisation means actual lift-off in the course of meditation and not simply a metaphor for a sensation of intense relaxation or lightness – evidenced by the many public exhibitions of 'hopping' arranged by the TM movement. TM's political arm, the Natural Law Party currently claims that yogic flying, when practised 'from the most refined and orderly level of individual consciousness' by the square root of 1% of a population, leads to a reduced crime rate.[33]

The TM movement's image has been evolving away from that of a science or secular therapy and towards that of an eastern religion. In the words of one authority: 'TM's emergence as a religious cult movement is related to the fall in initiations documented earlier ... No longer able to promise the material and social resources of many new recruits, the movement promised instead magical benefits symbolised by the defiance of physical nature through levitation ... The needs of dedicated TM teachers pressed toward more religion, not less'.[34] Levitation has traditionally been one of the *siddhis* or powers which were well known in yogic circles as far back as Patanjali. For him the possession of *siddhis* is a mixed blessing since 'the deployment of these powers presupposes that we pay attention to the external world and its concerns'.[35] This in turn militates against the Patanjali yoga's objective of disengagement from the world.

Transcendental Meditation has probably been the largest and most influential of the many Indian religious movements reaching western countries in recent times. Literally millions of westerners have taken up the practice of TM for some time at least. Many have found and continue to find in the practice a form of therapy for coping with stress and tension. The spiritual impact of TM includes those within the Christian churches who have been inspired by it to develop methods of centering prayer and Christian mantra meditation. The movement itself now seems destined to attract even fewer new adherents in the foreseeable future, for two reasons. The first is the growing realisation among the population at large that TM is indeed a religious movement rather than the non-sectarian science that it purports to be. Secondly, in the time since TM made its presence felt in the 1960s, there is far more 'competition' from alternative approaches to meditation and from other new religions. The future of TM seems likely to be in the form of a smaller, leaner and more overtly religious organisation. As one authority puts it: 'The decline left a solidly organised religious cult movement, undoubtedly one of the largest new religions in America'.[36]

Yogas of Sound and Light

This section looks at a number of movements which have over the past hundred years or so sprung from an ancient form of Indian spirituality known as the *Sant Mat* or the 'path of saints'. All of these groups believe that spiritual progress requires the personal aid of a living *sant* or spiritual Master.[1] The form of yoga which they practise is termed *suratshabd* yoga or 'yoga of the audible and visible life current'.[2] Within this tradition God is regarded primarily as Sound and secondly as Light. *Suratshabd* yoga – also termed 'yoga of sound and light' – aims to train the disciple in techniques of meditation that will enable him or her to 'hear the divine Sound' and 'see the divine Light'. However, these techniques are kept secret within the tradition and are revealed only to those who are judged to be 'ready' for them. Those who have been initiated into this yoga and have begun to experience the divine Light and Sound are said to possess 'the knowledge'.[3]

Movements in western countries that practise sound and light yoga include the Divine Light Mission of Guru Maharaj (more recently called Élan Vital), the Kripal Light Satsang and Eckankar. The Divine Light Mission is a Hindu sect, while the roots of Eckankar and Kripal Light spring from the Sikh tradition. These two movements however have their immediate origins in a modern religious movement, the Radha Soami tradition, that is highly influential both in India and in the west.

The Radha Soami Tradition

The Radha Soami movement is named after Soamiji Maharaj who founded it in Agra in 1861. Soamaji Maharaj systematised and made public spiritual teachings which though age-old, were first expounded by the *bhakti reformer Kabir (1440–1518). In the course of the past century an on-going splitting process has been at work, leading to the establishment of several groups of Radha Soamis. The largest of these has its headquarters at Beas in the Punjab. Its present living master, Maharaj Charan Singh presides over an estimated world following of one million. Most of these are Indians, though the movement also has a number of centres in western countries.

The classical English language source for the teachings of the Radha Soamis is *The Path of the Masters* by Julian Johnson. Johnson (1873–1939) was an American who went to India as a Baptist missionary. After some years he lost his faith in Christianity. His subsequent spiritual search took him through Rosicrucianism and Theosophy. In 1932 he was initiated into Radha Soami as a disciple of Sawan Singh, who presided over the Beas community between 1903 and 1948. Sawan was grandfather of the present incumbent, Charan Singh. Apparently, Sawan commissioned Johnson to reveal some (but not all) of the teaching of the Radha Soamis, which had up to then been kept secret.

Johnson's book, *The Path of the Masters* was first published in 1939. It gives insights not only into Radha Soami Beas, to which its author belonged, but to the entire tradition of *surat shabd*, which he rendered in English as 'audible life stream'. The Audible Life Stream is, he claimed, the oldest and only way to authentic 'self-realisation' or 'God-realisation'. Other religious systems, from the **vedas* onwards, constitute a deterioration from what went before and have only served to obscure true knowledge of the Life Stream. This knowledge can be learnt only from a spiritual master who is living in the flesh or at least who was living at the time of the disciple's initiation.[4] Johnson argues that knowledge of the life stream can be communicated only through the three senses of sight, hearing and touch.[5] Great spiritual masters have lived at various times in history, but those of previous centuries are unable to initiate us into the Life Stream. The fact that Jesus lived in the historical past is given by Johnson as the reason he abandoned the Christian Church in favour of the living tradition represented by Sawan Singh.

Johnson numbers the founders of the world's great religions among the masters. Pride of place, he tells us, must go to the leaders of the Sikh religion because its founder Guru Nanak and nine of his successors filled the role of genuine living masters. From his examination of the New Testament he concludes that Jesus was an outstanding living master who in his life-time had travelled to the Orient and had personal contact with the Audible Life Stream. Johnson in fact identifies the Audible Life Stream with the *Logos* ('Word') spoken of in St John's gospel.[6] However, the religion of Jesus was soon 'covered over with dogmas and superstitions' and was 'smothered, almost in the hour of its birth, by its over-enthusiastic nurses'.[7] In order to get in touch with what Jesus really taught, that is, the Audible Life Stream, Johnson urged the Christians of his time to sit at the feet of the master who was then living – namely his own teacher, Sawan Singh.[8]

Those who have been initiated into the Audible Life Stream by a living master are said to have 'knowledge' of God through the master.[9] These have the all-powerful Stream of Love to give life to their religion. This knowledge is very different from intellectual ideas produced by the mind which (it is believed) can so easily mislead us. The disciple must remember that 'this mind is his worst enemy, as well as his most useful instrument'.[10] Given this opinion of the human mind, it is not surprising that the tradition of the masters attaches little value to theology or any attempt to understand or gain information about God.[11]

Once the disciple has been initiated by the living master, he can begin the exercises of *surat shabd*. Sitting in meditation he focuses all of his attention on a point inside the head known as the *tisra til* or 'third eye'. One is to think of nothing at all – except the master – at this inner centre. After some time one moves on to *simran* or *smarana* ('remembering') which involves concentrating on some one object or phrase and mentally going over it again and again until it has become part of one's being. The next stage is 'closing the nine doors', that is withdrawing one's attention from the nine bodily openings – eyes, ears, nostrils, mouth, sex organ and rectum – and moving towards the centre.

As a result of persevering in these practices, certain experiences will start to occur. The student will begin to see flashes of light or hear sounds. Eventually the point will be reached when the soul has sufficient force to pass through 'the tenth door', that is, leave the body through 'an opening in the subtle body near the middle of the forehead'.[12] What happens after this as described by Johnson is an upward journey by the soul through various 'planes' of the 'astral zone'. This journey is accompanied by increased understanding, joy and spiritual power. The disciple will be met by the 'Radiant Form' of his spiritual master, who will lead him on to still higher zones. Soon the soul will begin to hear and be delighted by the music of the Audible Life Stream. With the master it will arrive in the Capital, the city of the 'thousand-petalled lotus'.[13]

It is claimed that the above series of exercises carries the student through 'the gates of death'.[14] He leaves his body in much the same way as a dying person does, except that he can come back into his body any moment he wishes. To the extent that a person is practised in *surat shabd* yoga, it is believed that he will enjoy mastery over the entire process of death and dying and will be freed from the need to reincarnate when he does finally discard his body.

KRIPAL LIGHT SATSANG INC.

Kripal Singh was a member of the Radha Soami community at Beas. Like Julian Johnson he too was a devoted follower of Sawan Singh. However, following Sawan's death Kripal broke away from Radha Soami, Beas to form his own movement, which he called the *ruhani satsang* or 'divine science of the soul'. In 1955 Kripal went on a lecture tour of the United States in the course of which he added many American disciples to his movement. One of these was Paul Twitchell who was later to found his own religion which he termed Eckankar.

Kripal Singh died in 1974. His successor Thakar Singh was recognised as Living Master within the *ruhani satsang*. This branch of *surat shabd* yoga, which Thakar has renamed 'Kripal Light Satsang', has continued to develop in the west. 'Light-house Schools' have been established in the United States, Mexico, Panama, Germany as well as India. In June 1988 Thakar issued guide-lines for 'spiritual homes' to supplement the work of the schools in which children from the ages of four to ten would be separated from their parents and supervised 24 hours a day. In this way, Thakar believes, these children will grow up to be 'missionaries of God'.[15]

In his addresses Thakar Singh makes frequent references to the Bible and in particular likes to quote sayings of Jesus such as: 'As you sow, so shall you reap'; 'I will never leave thee or forsake thee'; 'God is love' and 'where two or three are gathered together in my name, there am I in the midst of them'. In a video of one of his lectures the outline of a cross can be clearly seen in the background.

However, while Thakar's message may superficially resemble that of the Gospel, in reality it is drawn almost entirely from the *surat shabd* tradition and specifically from the teaching of his own guru, Kripal Singh.

The non-Christian character of Thakar Singh's spirituality is shown in the dualist view that he takes of human nature. He teaches that human beings are in essence souls, and not bodies. The practice of meditation under the guidance of a competent teacher is designed to put aside the veil of ignorance created by our ego and our mind and thus to realise our true nature as soul.

Kripal Light Satsang will reveal its meditative techniques only to those who are prepared to accept a long list of demanding pre-conditions. These include abstinence from meat, fish, eggs, alcohol, tea, coffee, drugs, smoking and sex. Thakar Singh quotes his teacher Kripal as saying 'spirituality is life; sexuality is death'. All alternative forms of meditation and other spiritual practices are ruled out, in particular the practices of *pranayama, *kundalini yoga, use of crystals, tarot, psychic activity, channelling and witchcraft. While initially a lesser time will suffice, meditation in the Kripal Light Satsang is to be practised for at least three hours daily. Thakar justifies this by quoting the words: 'Tithe your time to God'. Tithing or 'giving one tenth' is an ancient Judaeo-Christian religious principle.

Apart from daily meditation usually done in private, members of Kripal Light Satsang come together for communal meditation, singing and sometimes a spiritual lecture given by the living master or his representative. During some of these sessions the master gives spiritual initiation to selected students by touching their eyes, ears and head. Some disciples are said to hear inner sounds such as that of a harp or a flute and to see spectacular visions of sun, moon, stars, colours and circles of light. This is regarded as evidence of their having experience of 'the holy inner Light and Sound'.[16]

ECKANKAR

Paul Twitchell was born in Paducah, Kentucky. There is some uncertainty about his date of birth, but it is most probably sometime in 1908. Little is known about his early life apart from the fact that during the Second World War he served in the United States navy for a number of years. From his youth he seems to have been generally interested in spiritual matters and to have practised various forms of meditation. In 1950 he joined Swami Premananda's Self-Revelation Church of Absolute Monism in Washington, DC. It seems that the Swami personally asked him to leave the Church in 1955 for reasons that remain unclear.[17]

Twitchell was initiated into Kripal Singh's *Ruhani Satsang* later in 1955. He was a somewhat fickle disciple. While following Kripal Singh as his guru, he experimented freely with other spiritual movements including Ron Hubbard's Scientology. During this period he began to write articles and one book, *The Tiger's Fang*, the manuscript of which he sent to Kripal. Kripal however, refused to validate the spiritual attainments claimed by Twitchell in his book. There was a complete break in the relationship between the two men in 1963 or 1964. Twitchell next presented himself as the author of a new movement which he called 'Eckankar', a term which in Sanskrit means literally 'one oneness'.[18] Within a few years Eckankar was being hailed by many as the 'Ancient Science of Soul Travel'. In reality Twitchell was leading people to have 'out of the body' experiences or 'bilocation' as he preferred to call it. During these experiences the student might 'meet with' or 'hear the voice of' the 'living ECK Master' who was none other than Twitchell himself.

According to Twitchell the teachings of Eckankar were handed down through an unbroken line of ECK masters, of whom Twitchell himself was the 971st. He claimed to have spirit communication with his immediate predecessor, 'Rebazar Tars' who (he said) lived in Tibet in the fifteenth century. In October 1965 Tarz supposedly passed on the role of master to Twitchell.[19] Following his death in 1971 Twitchell was succeeded as living master number 972 by Darwin Gross. Gross's leadership was controversial. In 1984 he was displaced as Master by Harold Klemp whom Gross had in 1981 declared to be the 973rd living ECK master.[20]

In the United States and Europe Eckankar offers a more popularised version of Sound and Light yoga than the more traditional offshoots from the Radha Soami tradition. Its annual publication, the *Eck Mata Journal* is attractively edited and contains easy-to-read personal testimonies of people who claim to have been helped in various crisis situations by their ability to leave their bodies and allow themselves to be guided by 'the Living Eck Master'.

One basic Eckankar exercise involves silently chanting the syllable 'HU'. According to reports, HU is the sound that 'opens the tenth door' of the body and brings the practitioner out of his or her body and leads to a spiritual encounter with the 'Mahanta' or living Eck master. Another way to encounter the living master is said to be through paying attention to one's dreams. The presence of the living master realised in this way is believed to bring about many beneficial effects in a variety of different situations – sick or injured people have been healed, an African village was freed from evil spirits, people have been able to improve their typing or lose weight.[21]

The substance – as distinct from the presentation – of Eckankar's philosophy is derived almost totally from the *surat shabd* yoga tradition as expounded by Julian Johnson and Kripal Singh. Even the language Twitchell used in *The Tiger's Fang* is in places similar to passages from Julian Johnson's *The Path of the Masters* and *With a Great Master in India*.[22] This may have been a factor in Kripal Singh's refusal in 1963 to approve the publication of Twitchell's manuscript of *The Tiger's Fang*. It might also account for the continuing hostility between Eckankar and Kripal Light Satsang in particular.

THE DIVINE LIGHT MISSION

The Divine Light Mission is a guru movement within Hinduism, which like the groups mentioned above had its origins in northern India. In the 1930s its founder Shri Hans Ji Maharaj became a disciple of a saint known as Dada Guru. Hans Ji entered *samadhi* during meditation the day after his initiation. He succeeded Dada Guru as teacher after the latter's death and formally founded the Divine Light Mission around 1960. He died in 1966 and was succeeded in turn by his eight year-old son, Balyogeshwar who declared himself to be the 'Perfect Master' or Guru Maharaj Ji.

During the 1970s, the Divine Light Mission under the direction of the charismatic Guru Maharaj became a world-wide organisation adding some 50,000 United States disciples to its ranks, plus thousands more in Europe. However, in 1974 the marriage of the sixteen year-old guru to his American-born secretary precipitated a split in Maharaj Ji's family and in the movement. Balyogeshwar's mother and his elder brother Bal Bhagavan objected to Maharaj's worldly lifestyle and had themselves recognised as leaders of the Divine Light Mission by the majority of its Indian members. The western followers for the most part sided with Maharaj Ji. In the early 1980s Maharaj changed the name of his part of the movement to 'Élan Vital' and began to adopt a more western and less Indian profile.

Those who take initiation into the Divine Light Mission are said to have received 'the knowledge'. The term 'knowledge' in this sense means the experience or realisation of God that the Guru offers and not any kind of rational information. For followers of Maharaj Ji, the derisive term 'mind' is used to describe all of one's ideas, logical processes, ambitions, preoccupations, attachments and errors – everything in short that one is conscious of and which does not come from the perfect master. The Divine Light Mission/Élan Vital is thus fundamentally anti-intellectual and unlike the schools of the Radha Soami tradition, among others, has never produced a body of literature outlining its beliefs and practices.

Followers of Maharaj Ji are expected to spend two hours daily in a form of yogic meditation based on four specific techniques which are not supposed to be revealed to non-initiates. From the testimony of ex-members however, the 'four techniques' are known to be as follows:[23]

(i) *Seeing the Divine Light*

To do this one begins by concentrating on a point in the groove between the eyes. Within the yogic tradition this point is known as the 'third eye'. After some time one places the right index finger against the forehead, and the thumb and middle finger pressing gently on the corners of the eyeballs. Most people (including non-initiates) who do this exercise are able to see white light at the point of concentration.

(ii) *Hearing the Divine Music*

This requires that one sit very still, block the ears with ones' thumbs and concentrate on what one can hear within the right ear. People variously report hearing ringing bell-like sounds or the music of their favourite instruments.

(iii) *Tasting the Divine Nectar*

The disciple curls his tongue up and back until the tip reaches the hollow behind the roof of the mouth. In this way one is supposed to find the passage where 'the divine nectar' drips down.

(iv) *Hearing the Word, the Holy Name of God*

Listening to himself or herself breathing deeply, the disciple is taught to 'hear' the name of God in the sound of the breathing. This is believed to tune the meditator to the primordial Sound that lies behind all speech and sound.

NON-THINKING AND MIND-CONTROL

The schools of yoga mentioned in this chapter keep their techniques secret from non-initiates. They believe theirs to be a timeless form of yoga which has been passed down orally and in secret from master to disciple. Only in recent times is their teaching being revealed to humanity at large – or rather, to those people in whatever part of the world who are ready to receive it. In point of fact many of their practices were already described in a series of medieval documents known as *Yoga Upanishads*.

These movements actively discourage their disciples from using their minds and particularly their critical faculty – and therein lies a danger. Systematically cultivating a non-thinking attitude towards one's beliefs and the way one lives one's life, carries with it the risk of leaving oneself open to having one's thinking shaped and one's life controlled by another person's thinking. Eckankar and Élan Vital in particular are among the groups that the 'anti-cult movement' has accused of controlling the minds of its members in an unethical way, with serious psychological consequences in some cases.

KUNDALINI YOGA AND SWAMI MUKTANANDA

Kundalini is a symbolic term that occurs in a number of important centuries-old *tantric* yoga texts. It refers to the energy that is believed to lie dormant at the base of the spine in every human being. It is most commonly visualised as a coiled serpent. The form of yoga that is used to activate the potential *kundalini* energy within each person is called *kundalini* yoga. The same energy is sometimes conceived of as a goddess of power named *shakti* – *shakti* being the Sanskrit for 'power'.

Initiation into *kundalini* yoga generally takes place in the controlled environment of a yoga ashram. It can be a long drawn out process involving many years' practice of yogic exercises, meditation and *pranayama* under the guidance of an experienced teacher.[1] But there are alternative traditions which are more spontaneous and less structured than this. These are represented in the writings of Gopi Krishna (1903–1984), as well as movements like Sahaja Yoga founded by Mataji Nirmala Devi (b. 1923) and the Siddha Yoga Dham movement, founded by Swami Muktananda – the subject of this chapter.

The Siddha yoga ashram in Oakland, California and its sister ashram at South Fallsburg, New York were established by Swami Muktananda following his visits to the United States in the 1960s. During the years that followed Siddha yoga has touched the lives of many, including a number of celebrities such as singers John Denver and Diana Ross, and film actress Olivia Hussey. In addition, some of Muktananda's disciples have gone on to become leaders of independent religious movements in their own right. These include Richard Alpert (Ram Dass), Albert Rudolf (Swami Rudrananda) and Franklyn Jones (Da Free John). Since Muktananda's death in 1982, the Siddha yoga movement has been overseen by his disciple, Gurumayi Chidvilasananda. Gurumayi, like Muktananda before her, is based at the main Siddha yoga ashram in Ganeshpuri near Bombay, India.

Entering the Oakland ashram from the canopied side-walk, one gets the impression of a hotel reception area complete with counter and 'Registration' sign. On the right hand side is the 'Amrta' vegetarian restaurant. Towards the rear of the ashram and approached through a patioed garden is the Chant and Meditation Cave – a room so dimly lit as to require a few moments of adjustment to its atmosphere, which is enhanced by the smell of incense and the soft recorded chanting of the mantra: *Om Namah Shivaya* meaning 'hail the name of *shiva'. There are cushions for the meditator's comfort and the walls are lined with bronze or brass statuettes of various Hindu deities and some life-size black and white photos of gurus from the past. The most striking presence in the room however, is a life-sized coloured picture of the late Swami Muktananda. His figure presides over a low altar on which are laid oil lamps and a bronze statue of *shiva nataraja depicting the four-armed god in a dancing pose.

The spacious, carpeted assembly hall has a notice prominently displayed on its door: 'No photographs, recording or note taking in the hall'. It is here that the popular 'chanting nights' and other rituals take place. It is the largest area in the ashram. Shoes must be removed before one is allowed to enter. Its interior resembles that of a modern church building. In place of an altar, there is a throne seat above which are placed large illuminated photographs of Muktananda and the remarkably young-looking and strikingly beautiful Gurumayi. The right hand wall is lined with large black and white photos of a succession of *siddha yoga gurus going back more than a century. The chanting nights attract hundreds of people, mainly aged between 25 and 40 and mostly female. Many are committed devotees and position themselves in various postures of veneration before one or other of the images of 'Baba' (Muktananda) throughout the hall.

LIFE IN THE ASHRAM

Each of the two American Siddha yoga ashrams is open both to casual visitors and those who want to stay for longer periods. For ashram residents the day begins as early as 3.30 am. From then until 'Lights Out' there are six hours of religious exercises divided between meditation, worship, lectures and chanting. Another six and a half hours are devoted to *guruseva* or 'service of the guru', which means house-keeping and other work.

In addition to the daily schedule, each of the ashrams offers a wide variety of courses. These include 'The Intensive', which is a one-day $350 programme during which participants 'receive the rare gift of the Siddhas, Shaktipat, the inner awakening of (the) divine Kundalini energy'.[2] There are also less costly courses in meditation, hatha yoga and Indian music. In general the Siddha yoga ashrams are busy centres of spirituality with exceptionally well organised programmes of worship.

During a typical service, as the congregation take their places, the stage is set by some gently chanted mantras led by a small choir backed up by an Indian music ensemble. During the singing of the opening hymn (the Hindi words of which are displayed on a large screen), a woman wearing a sari goes up the aisle with a tray containing flowers, a lighted flame and smoking incense sticks. She moves the tray slowly in a circular motion in front of the throne. This gesture of worship is termed *arati* and is universal in Hindu temple worship.

The talks that follow combine instruction with personal testimony, punctuated by lengthy mantra chanting sessions. Typical of the testimonies would be that of a man who spoke about his 'Intensive'. During the weekend he had experienced an explosion of energy at the base of his spine. This he understood to be the 'awakening of *kundalini*' and for him a life-changing event. A woman lawyer explained how through meditation, she had managed to advance her career to the extent of becoming a judge. For her the *kundalini experience caused her heart to open up like a flower. This was accompanied by weeping and a great sense of joy. Afterwards she felt more 'connected' – a term much used by Muktananda devotees.

The climax of each service is usually a video of a talk by Gurumayi, during which she quotes and chants in Sanskrit short passages from Hindu Scriptures. In one of these she summed up her address with a phrase which she repeated emphatically: 'God is in you as your own self'. She ended her presentation by leading both her video and real audiences into a chanting of *Om namah shivaya* – having first explained that in worshipping *shiva one is simply worshipping the Self within.

SWAMI MUKTANANDA

Swami Muktananda was born in 1908 of wealthy and pious Hindu parents in Mysore state (present day Karnataka). Before his birth his mother, earnestly seeking a son, had been praying incessantly the mantra *Om namah shivaya*. When the child was born he was given the name 'Krishna'. At the age of fifteen he had a chance encounter with a wandering mystic named Swami Nityananda. Nityananda embraced him, stroked him on the cheeks and suddenly walked away. The boy 'felt a strange magnetic spell', the impact of which remained with him for the rest of his life.

Soon afterwards Krishna walked away penniless from home. His extraordinary spiritual journey was to continue for more than thirty years. Among the many Hindu saints with whom he had contact during this period were Zipruanna and Harigiri Baba. Zipruanna healed Muktananda's persistent headaches by means of a curious remedy. He had him sit on his lap and then licked his head. Later, Muktananda used water that had been poured over Zipruanna's foot, to cure a woman with advanced tuberculosis. In 1947 Muktananda again fell under the charm of Swami Nityananda and for the next eight years lived with him in his ashram at Ganeshpuri near Bombay.[3]

KUNDALINI INITATION

It was at Ganeshpuri that Muktananda was fully initiated into the *siddha* yoga tradition. According to Muktananda's own account Swami Nityananda performed a series of symbolic actions including touching Muktananda with his body, gazing intently into his eyes, and giving him his own sandals. He also initiated him formally into the mantra *Om namah shivaya*, explaining to him that its true meaning is 'I am Shiva'. Muktananda understood that Nityananda had given him 'the insight that all is one Self'.[4]

Muktananda subsequently moved out to a little hut on his own to undertake a period of intense meditation practice. There he had a succession of disturbing experiences. These included horrific visions of screaming demon-like creatures and of the whole world being destroyed by fire.[5] He found himself on occasion spontaneously writhing and hissing like a snake or alternately roaring like a lion, a tiger or a camel.[6] At one stage his meditation was disrupted by the alluring vision of a beautiful naked woman which remained in front of him whether his eyes were open or closed. This was particularly distressing for him because of his conviction that every kind of sickness and weakness that afflicts human beings is caused by the 'waste of sexual fluid, sensuality and most of all, irregular living'.[7] He was tempted to give up his spiritual practice altogether. However, meetings with Harigiri Baba and Zipruanna helped him recognise that, as a result of his initiation by Nityananda, he was simply going through the awakening of *kundalini. Among the blessings which would result from this would be the sublimation of his sexual energies into increased powers of memory and intelligence as well as the ability to love more intensely.[8]

For Muktananda there were less alarming and more pleasing aspects to the arousal of *kundalini. His body would move automatically into various classical yoga postures such as the lotus and half-lotus.[9] He heard 'sweet and melodious divine music' in his inner ear – the *nada of yogic tradition.[10] He smelt sweet fragrances that seemed not of this world.[11] He had visions of surreal scenes and distant places that he had never visited, and saw 'divine light' which changed colour as his spiritual practice advanced. According to Muktananda, the most significant episode in all of this was signalled by the appearance of 'a tiny blue dot (which) illuminated everything in every direction'.[12] This was his first mystical encounter with what he described as a 'Blue Pearl', which on occasion grew into a 'Blue Person'. When in his meditation he 'passed inside the Blue Pearl', Muktananda believed that he had achieved the fulfilment of his pilgrimage – the final realisation of God: *advaita or non-duality.[13] He became convinced that the self of every human being was an integral part of God, or even identical with God, so that one can say: 'He is I, I am He', or 'You are God, God is in you'.[14]

SIDDHA YOGA

The spiritual path taught by Swami Muktananda has ancient roots within the yogic traditions of India. Muktananda used the term 'siddha yoga' to describe his form of yoga. He declared himself to be 'a follower

of the Siddha Path' and heir to the secret tradition of the *siddhas, handed down over centuries from guru to disciple.[15] The word *siddha (meaning 'perfect' or 'accomplished') refers to the perfect master who has attained enlightenment and is fully Self-realised. However, in popular yoga tradition a *siddha master is one who possesses magical power (*siddhi). In particular the term is seen as referring to the *siddha sect, which
flourished particularly between the eighth and twelfth centuries. This
followed a synthesis of the spiritual teachings both of Hinduism and
Buddhism and added to them many elements of alchemy and popular
magic. Yogic folklore records a number of famous *siddha yogis, including the Buddhist Nagarjuna (second century AD) and Gorakhnath, re-
puted to be the inventor of hatha yoga. Gorakhnath and his teacher,
Matsyendranath founded the cult of the kanphatas or 'split ears' (so
called because they pierce their ears with large rings in the belief that
this enabled them to acquire certain magical powers). The kanphatas,
who still survive in parts of Bengal and Maharashtra, were responsible
for some of the most famous hatha yoga texts, including the Hatha yoga
Pradipika and the Gheranda Samhita.[16]

One of the characteristic features of *siddha yoga is its curious process of initiation called *shaktipat or 'descent of the Power'. This can take
place through the touch or even the mere glance of a guru. Examples of
*shaktipat can be read in the above account of the young Muktananda's
meetings with his teachers, Zipruanna and Nityananda. There are numerous recorded instances of Muktananda himself conferring 'the descent of the Power' on some of his followers.[17] *Shaktipat is designed to
trigger 'the inner awakening of (the) divine Kundalini energy'.[18]

Inner experiences of melodious sounds and visions of light play an
important part in *siddha yoga. These latter can sometimes amount to a
kaleidescope of brilliant colours. Particular significance is attached to
the vision during meditation of a blue pearl, which the Oakland
ashram's literature describes as 'the Self in the form of light'. Apart from
Muktananda and his followers, commentators on the yogic tradition
see a spiritual purpose in such experiences. These inner visions can be
viewed as dress rehearsals for the encounter with the Light of lights.[19]
Similarly, listening to the inner *nada or 'sound' is regarded as a prelude
to identifying with the Self.[20] The sound and light phenomena are not to

be cultivated for their own sakes, but simply as stepping stones along the way to enlightenment.

CONCLUSION

In 1982, the year of Muktananda's death, some thirty of his followers accused him of regular and long-standing sexual misconduct with many of the movement's young female devotees and left the movement. One senior member, Stan Trout, who was known as Swami Abhyananda, wrote a widely publicised letter of resignation to Muktananda in which he accused him of sexually exploiting girls as young as thirteen under the pretext of *tantric* initiation. In addition Trout accused Muktananda of threatening, harassing and spreading lies about several members of the movement including Trout himself, who had begun to divulge the leader's sexual activity.[21]

The Swami's sexual behaviour has not been the only cloud to hang over the *siddha* yoga movement in recent years. Muktananda's appointed co-successors – Gurumayi Chidvilasananda and her brother, Swami Nityananda (named after Muktananda's own guru) had a falling out. Gurumayi won the ensuing power struggle in 1985.[22]

The question could be asked as to whether the crises within this movement are simply the results of human weakness or whether the seeds of the problem can be found within the *siddha* yoga teachings themselves – or at least the version of them that Muktananda taught. His message was that enlightenment came about not through austerities or difficult yogic practices, but simply through *guru kripa* – the 'guru's grace' – given during the initiation ritual of *shaktipat*: 'Do not do anything. Do not use any methods or techniques. Just sit down and meditate. How does the guru's grace reach one? Well, Gurudev's *shakti* catches them (devotees) like a strong infection'. With regard to morals, he stated: 'Divine Reality pervades everything. Even what appear to be opposites are in fact expressions of the same Reality'.[23] Muktananda's emphasis on 'not doing anything' appears to be a form of Quietism – a movement that made its appearance within the Christian tradition in the Middle Ages and again in the seventeenth century. On occasion it was accompanied by questionable moral behaviour.

An authentic mystical pilgrimage has traditionally been thought of as leading to greater detachment on the part of the pilgrim, a greater ability to accept pain, discomfort and 'dryness' for the sake of a greater good. There are some indications that the spontaneous *kundalini* practice of Muktananda did not always facilitate this kind of holy indifference. His progress seems to have been fuelled to a degree by a need for sense fulfilment as indicated by his own words: 'I began to be addicted to meditation'; 'I was greedy for visions'; 'I could not bear any noise ...'[24] This contrasts somewhat with the moral and ascetic challenge found for instance in the spiritualities of the *Bhagavad Gita* and the Gospels.

More fundamental questions can be raised as to the nature of the experiences that Muktananda (and his disciples after him) have had during the awakening of *kundalini*. Do these experiences constitute a genuine spiritual awakening, or are they on the other hand signs of a disturbed psyche? Could they even be the result of demonic influence – as has been suggested by at least one critic?[25]

Muktananda's Siddha yoga invites the would-be practitioner to embark on a path that is demanding in terms of service to the guru and the temple, non-specific in terms of moral requirements, and spectacular in its promise of inner meditative experience. However, as to where that path leads, serious and significant questions remain unanswered.

THE POLITICAL YOGA OF
ANANDA MARG

Yoga is traditionally associated with a turning inwards and away from 'the world', and its methods are primarily designed for the inner journey. In recent years however, some yogis have left the confinement of their ashrams and become involved in society and its struggles. *Tantric techniques in particular have been harnessed to give energy to politically motivated groups. The best-known example of this in recent times is the Japanese Aum Shinri Kyo cult, notorious for its sarin gas attack on the Tokyo underground in March 1995. Though outside of India, this group and its leader, Shoko Asahara used *shiva, the Indian god of destruction, as its principal ikon. Asahara had travelled to the Himalayas to learn *tantric techniques such as 'yogic flying' which he attempted to teach to his followers. Devotees of Aum Shinri Kyo spent much time in meditation and chanting.

Despite the above, Asahara's movement remains complex, with elements drawn from many diverse sources. Ananda Marg, the subject of this chapter, is a more clear-cut example of the application of traditional *tantric technique to political objectives.

Ananda Marg in Sanskrit means literally 'Path of Joy'. The organisation of this name was founded in 1954–1955 by Prabhat Ranjan Sarkar (1921–1990) – known to his disciples as Anandamurti. Sarkar was the son of an accounts clerk at the Jamalpur Railway workshop in west Bengal. After finishing school he went to college in Calcutta. While studying there he was initiated into the practice of *tantric yoga, probably by his uncle, the Indian nationalist leader, Subhas Chandra Bose (1897–1945).[1] Bose was a radical who collaborated with both the Germans and the Japanese with a view to ridding India of British rule. Following unconfirmed reports of his death in an air crash, rumours about his being alive have persisted. Pictures of Bose have found their place among the images of Hindu gods in many Indian homes, particularly in Bengal. Today, for many Indian nationalists he occupies the role of mythical hero.[2] Bose's radical politics may have been a significant influence in the shaping of Ananda Marg's political philosophy.

On completing his BA degree, Sarkar returned to Jamalpur to become a clerical worker at the railway workshop, a position he held for about thirty years. At the same time he continued to be a regular and committed practitioner of *tantric yoga. In time he began to teach *tantric practices to others, but with an economic and political agenda added on. Sarkar had little regard for any form of yoga which did not seek to arouse spiritual awareness in others as well as in oneself. He used the term 'spiritual capitalists' to describe those who go after personal Self-realisation without also practising service to humanity.[3] This combining of yoga with social action is a characteristic of the Ananda Marg movement.

At its height in the late 1960s Ananda Marg had grown into a huge organisation with a host of affiliate wings in almost every region of the world. Even today it has several hundred thousand followers and continues to recruit new members both in India and in many western countries. The movement has a number of affiliated organisations devoted to social, economic and political development. AMURT (the Ananda Marg Universal Relief Team) works on disaster relief and social uplift in poorer areas of India and elsewhere. RU (Renaissance Universal) aims to bring about a world-wide intellectual awakening through discussion groups, clubs, research and publishing. WWD (Women's Welfare Department) runs schools, self-help centres and other activities with a view to making women economically independent of men. The principal affiliate and one which Sarkar set up very soon after founding Ananda Marg is the PROUT organisation which has its world headquarters in Copenhagen – of which more in the next section.

In recent years a significant part of Ananda Marg's activities has been running children's schools and orphanages. Under the name of the Sunrise Education Trust, the Marg runs schools for children in North London, Birmingham and Stoke Newington in Britain. It recently applied for planning permission for a centre in Co. Clare in the west of Ireland to cater for up to 200 people.[4] There is usually a spiritual as well as a social agenda behind Ananda Marg's developmental projects. This has landed the organisation in controversy in Romania when it was reported that children under the age of seven were being covertly introduced to Hindu meditation practices. It was also alleged that sick orphaned children were having their normal medication replaced by a mainly homeopathic and strictly vegetarian diet.[5]

PROGRESSIVE UTILISATION THEORY

The term PROUT (Progressive Utilisation Theory) refers to the social, economic and political philosophy which Sarkar developed in opposition to both capitalism and communism. For him a major drawback with capitalism is its failure to guarantee employment for all, whereas in 'PROUT's collective economic system, full employment will be maintained by progressively reducing working hours as the introduction of appropriate scientific technology increases production'.[6] One of communism's main drawbacks is that without 'a sense of personal ownership people do not labour hard or care for any property'.[7] Both capitalism and communism fail in that they lead to an over-centralised economy, with all major decisions being made from one or a few centres of power. PROUT, on the other hand, advocates a network of localised economies, involving a high degree of co-operative enterprise. It is only in this way, Sarkar believed, that a steadily increasing standard of amenities could be achieved for all the world's peoples. According to his theory, as local economic units become more prosperous, they will tend to merge with other units. This process will lead to the emergence of a world government which will in turn promote the integrated development of each socio-economic unit.[8]

Sarkar believed in the need for an 'all-round spiritual revolution in individual and collective life under the leadership of a group of accomplished and idealistic leaders'.[9] He used the term *sadvipra* to describe the kind of leader he had in mind. A *sadvipra* is a person who is highly developed in all three levels of human life, namely: physical, mental and spiritual. Sarkar believed that such persons alone were fit to hold political power, but unfortunately rarely got themselves elected even in the modern democracies. In his earlier speeches and writings at least, he maintained that force should be used if necessary to bring the *sadvipras* to power.[10] It is believed that Sarkar retracted this view in his later years, though not before violence both against and on the part of Ananda Marg had become a sad reality.

Ananda Marg was the victim of violence as early as 1967 when the Marg's international headquarters at Purulia in west Bengal was the subject of an attack by 5,000 armed tribesmen. Five Margis were killed. The attack appears to have been instigated by local communists who had shown animosity towards the Marg – probably viewing it as a potentially serious revolutionary rival. In 1969 and 1971 there were several more violent encounters between Marxists and Margis – with the Indian police tending to side with the Marxists. By now the police had become suspicious of the Marg due to reports that they were preaching secession and that the organisation's objective was to capture political power through an armed revolution. In June 1971 police raided Sarkar's quarters in Ranchi and found unlicensed firearms, bags full of bombs, human skulls and blood-soaked clothes – indications that the Marg too was prepared to act violently.

The most dramatic events concerning Ananda Marg during this period were internal. One of Sarkar's closest collaborators, Madhvananda – whose real name is Gour Mazumdar – had been among those arrested in the wake of the arms find. While in custody he confessed that on Sarkar's orders he had brutally murdered 18 defectors from the movement. In December 1971 Sarkar and four of his followers were arrested and charged with the murder of six ex-Margis. The subsequent trial focused international attention on Ananda Marg after a number of disciples immolated themselves in protest against Sarkar's detention. Despite the protests, Sarkar and his four co-accused were convicted and on 29 November 1976 they were sentenced to life imprisonment. They were however, acquitted of these charges and released in 1978.

The period of Sarkar's detention had been marked by violent outrages for which Ananda Marg members would serve lengthy jail sentences long after his release. Some of the most dramatic acts were carried out by western followers of Sarkar. In November 1978 three Margis were jailed in Britain for attempting to murder India House officials. In August 1979 three Australian Margis were sentenced to 16 years imprisonment for conspiring to murder the leader of a right wing Australian political party – and also a number of police officers. In a major incident in 1982 seventeen Indian members of Ananda Marg were savagely killed in a series of orchestrated attacks in the streets of Calcutta. No one has been found guilty of these killings.

DANCE OF DEATH

In 1983 the Ananda Marg was in the news when the Indian Supreme Court upheld a police ban on the public performance of a Margi ritual dance known as the *tandav*. The Margis had claimed that the *tandav* dance was an integral part of their religion, though in fact its practice was introduced into the movement only in 1966, eleven years after Ananda Marg was founded.

The word *tandav* literally means 'frantic dancing'. The dance itself is a highly energetic rhythmical jumping exercise and may be practised only by men. With both arms extended, the dancer holds in his right hand a knife, sword, stick or trident – which Margis view as symbols of life. In his left hand he holds the symbol of death which can be a burning torch, a snake or a human skull. If a Margi has difficulty finding a real skull or snake, then plastic substitutes may be used. During the dance the participants repeatedly shout out the Marg's most popular mantra: *Baba nam kevalam* (literally 'the name of the father only'– the father in this case being Sarkar').[11] Groups of Margis had been regularly performing the *tandav* in the streets of Calcutta, using real skulls and daggers. It was displays such as these that the police wanted to ban.

While the Marg's use of the *tandav* is recent, the dance itself derives from a centuries-old tradition that is rich in sombre symbolism. An old *tantric* story speaks of *shiva*'s grief at the death of his wife Sati. *Shiva* 'wandered over the earth dancing madly with Sati's dead body on his shoulder'.[12] The god *shiva* is commonly represented in medieval sculpture as a four-armed dancer on the back of a much smaller prostrate human figure. For some recent commentators, this image symbolises the balance of creative and destructive forces in the universe. 'According to Hindu belief, all life is part of a great rhythmic process of creation and destruction, of death and rebirth ...'[13] Traditionally however, *shiva* is simply 'the destroyer of the universe',[14] the role of creation and conservation being assigned respectively to *brahma* and *vishnu*. While not being without some benign features, *shiva* is frequently portrayed 'as lurking in inauspicious places such as battlefields and burial grounds'.[15]

Burial grounds and crematoria provide the setting for another ritual of ancient *tantric* origin which is practised by some members of the movement. On new moon nights just before midnight the Margi sits down to meditate, having first placed a human skull behind his back. He then places another skull on his lap and begins meditating using *japa* beads (a form of Hindu rosary).[16] This practice links the Ananda Marg to some of the most unorthodox Hindu sects, such as the *aghoris*.

IMMOLATION

The extent to which rank and file members of Ananda Marg were prepared to suffer while their leader was on trial and in prison is an indication of the veneration in which they held him. The name by which they know him – *Anandamurti* – means literally 'form or incarnation of joy'. While Sarkar's biodata is well known, his disciples view him as more than merely human. A number of stories concerning his childhood have taken shape within the movement. These have a legendary or mythological quality about them. One describes how the four year-old Prabhat used to be carried from his bed at nighttime by a strong wind to be placed in front of the god *shiva*, who then taught him all the complicated *shivamantras*.[17] The point of this anecdote is to help explain Sarkar's more than human understanding, in which his followers have an unshakeable belief. Many Margis believe that Sarkar could speak every language in the world, that every word he spoke was infallibly true and that he was in fact God incarnate, of equal status with Krishna, Buddha, Mohammed or Christ.[18] In their own words 'the Guru and the Supreme Consciousness are the same'.[19] Identifying one's guru with God is not unusual within Hindu sects. However, the lengths to which Margis have been prepared to go in their service of the guru calls for some specific explanation.

One of the seven Margis who died as a result of setting fire to themselves, in protest against Sarkar's arrest and imprisonment, was Didi Asitiima Brci. Before her death in June 1978, she left a written testimony in which she compared the 'persecution' of Sarkar to that which was undergone by great religious leaders such as Christ, Krishna, Ramakrishna and Mohammed. More significantly she stated that a peaceful and happy human society could come about only by means of *'non-compromising* struggle against immorality with a one-pointed mind towards our very goal of life, the infinite realm of love and peace' *(italics mine).*[20] The language used here is highly significant and gives clues as to how these young Margis reached such a state of fanaticism that they were willing even to immolate themselves out of devotion to their guru. These clues will be followed up in the next section.

YOGA FOR ACTION

The westerner who encounters the Ananda Marg is likely to do so as a result of answering an advertisement or reading an attractively packaged brochure for a course in meditation or yoga postures. The initial impression is of a somewhat innocuous yoga-meditation group, little different from many others of the 'yoga for health' variety. However, on the Margi agenda, yoga or **tantra* – for them the two terms appear to be interchangeable – includes diet and ethical training as well as postures and meditation. In fact, they attempt to put into practice all eight limbs of yoga as described by Patanjali. The aim of the Ananda Marg's **tantra* is 'union with unqualified and limitless Consciousness – a state beyond the inhibiting ego and its segmentation of reality'.[21] This traditional Hindu approach to spirituality is accompanied by a warning of one's responsibility not to exclusively focus on one's own inner development. Spiritually developed people must remain involved in social activity in order to challenge corruption, exploitation and other socially harmful activities.[22]

The implementation of this programme depends on a disciplined life including twice or – for full-time members – four times daily meditation sessions. The favoured type of meditation is that which uses an *ishta* or 'chosen' mantra integrated with the meditator's breathing pattern. There are also *dharmacakra* or group meditation sessions which begin and end with a chanted mantra. All of these practices are to be done strictly under the direction of an *acharya* or religious teacher who initiates new members into the practice. *Acharyas* are appointed by someone higher up in the movement – ultimately by the Guru himself. How this yogic programme has the potential to end disastrously is indicated in the terms 'one-pointed' and 'non-compromising' used by Didi Asitiima Brci in her final testimony.

The term 'one-pointedness' (*ekagrata* in Sanskrit) is widespread throughout yogic literature going back as far as Patanjali. However, its application within yoga has almost always been limited to the concentration of body, mind and spirit required for the successful practice of meditation. The aim of traditional yogic meditation is disengagement from society, from one's own body and psychological processes in order the better to experience the true inner Self in utter solitude. In other words, main-stream yoga focuses the entire range of human energies inwards on oneself. The Ananda Marg approach utilises the same techniques but with an external as well as an internal agenda.

The Marg summarises its spiritual practices in a series of rules which they refer to as the '16 Points' The first eight of these points are concerned with physical health, hygiene and diet. Point Nine, 'spiritual practice' deals with yoga postures, ethical behaviour and social norms. Points Ten to Thirteen begin with the words 'Non-compromising strictness regarding ...' and apply this respectively to one's guru, ideology, rules of conduct and 'the Supreme Command'. The command in question applies to daily meditation, the yogic moral code and leading others along 'the Path of Righteousness'. The consequences of failure to obey the Command are spelt out: '... in the next life the mind will revert into an animal form ... This descent into animal life lasts a long time as animals cannot make any conscious efforts towards spirituality'.[23]

The age-old techniques of yoga have over the centuries shown themselves to be remarkably powerful instruments in bringing about psychological and spiritual transformation within the individual. The Ananda Marg departed from tradition by extracting these techniques from the world of spirituality and using them as tools of radical politics. And it is not the only political movement in contemporary India to have done so.[24] Perhaps yogic practices can and hopefully will be used successfully for social and political improvement. Unfortunately, for some of Anandamurti's followers that has not proven to be the case. Giving an outward twist to the inward-focusing, 'one-pointed' power of yoga and applying this with 'non-compromising strictness' in the political arena as they did, resulted in violence and death.

RAJA YOGA AND THE BRAHMA KUMARIS

The entire yoga culture of India has for two millenia been inspired by the *ashtanga* or 'eight-limbed' path of Patanjali. *Asana* (posture) and *pranayama* (breath control), the third and fourth of the eight limbs were developed within the context of *hatha*, *tantric* and *kundalini* yogas. These disciplines however, generally have beliefs very different from Patanjali's. Yoga movements which base themselves on the philosophy of Patanjali are relatively rare. Among such movements with an outreach in the west, the outstanding example is the Brahma Kumaris World Spiritual University, the subject of this chapter.

ONE MILLION MINUTES OF PEACE
In August 1986 a high-powered international advertising campaign was launched looking for support for the observance of a minute's silence for peace at midday on 16 September of that year. During the month that followed people were asked to donate as much time as possible to holding in their minds 'positive thoughts of peace'. They were also invited to fill up and send in to a prescribed address a donation form indicating the amount of time they would pledge to 'positive thoughts', 'meditation'or 'prayer'. The project was given the title 'The Million Minutes of Peace' (MMOP for short). Its launch took the form of large-scale public meetings led by well-known artists, scientists, politicians, media and sports personalities – as well as religious leaders of all faiths – in many countries. The event was an organisational *tour de force* that took many different forms. The minute of silence was announced and observed at a tennis match in Sydney between Boris Becker and Ivan Lendl. At midday on 16 September the Hong Kong stock exchange stopped all dealings for one minute. A pause during Church services was widely observed in the Philippines. Minutes of peace were donated during the Frankfurt Book Fair. In Britain Queen Elisabeth and the Archbishop of Canterbury joined in the minute's silence, while most of Ireland's contribution of minutes was collected by

the *Irish Catholic* newspaper. It was estimated that the appeal reached 88 countries and that over one billion minutes of peace were 'gathered'.[1] However, MMOP was also remarkable for another reason.

MMOP was supported by well-known public figures and sponsors in each of the countries in which it took place. However, the principal organisers of the event were not those sitting on public platforms or listed on headed note-paper, most of whom learnt of the event only a matters of weeks beforehand. The planning and administration of the Million Minutes of Peace project was initiated in India, at the headquarters of the Brahma Kumaris World Spiritual University (BKWSU) at Mount Abu in Rajasthan. Delegates from over 50 countries who had attended an international peace conference there, returned to their countries and began organising the event.

The United Nations presented seven Peace Messenger Awards to the Brahma Kumaris for their work in organising 'The Million Minutes of Peace' project.[2] These awards were but a few of many tokens of recognition that the UN has accorded BKSWU. In 1984 the Secretary-General of the UN, Perez de Cuellar presented BKSWU with a peace medal. BKSWU has enjoyed consultative status with UNESCO since 1983 and with UNICEF since 1988. It is the only religious organisation accredited to participate in the UN Economic and Social Council.

MMOP is not the only international outreach to have been organised by BKWSU. In 1988 it launched a movement called Global Co-operation to promote understanding between nations, communities and peoples. In 1989 the Global Hospital and Research Centre was established by BKSWU at Mount Abu. This focuses on a holistic approach to health and healing in a spiritual environment.

What is BKWSU? The next section will look at this institution and the dedicated group that operate BKSWU – the Brahma Kumaris, a religious movement whose philosophy and spiritual practices are rooted in one of India's most ancient yogic traditions, the *raja* yoga philosophy outlined by Patanjali two thousand years ago.[3]

HISTORY

The Brahma Kumaris World Spiritual University *(kumari* means 'girl' or 'unmarried woman')* was founded in Karachi in 1936 by Dada Lekhraj

(1877–1969), a business man who devoted all his wealth to the under-taking. Lekhraj is reported to have received a number of visions during one of which his body became illumined and a voice not his own was heard to say: 'I am the Blissful self, I am Shiva ... I am the Knowledgeful self ... I am the Luminous self ...' Lekhraj's mainly female followers – who were to be known as Brahma Kumaris – believed that *shiva had entered his body to empower him to inaugurate a new world order. The original group of 300 Brahma Kumaris lived as a self-sufficient com-munity, spending their time in intense spiritual study, meditation and self-transformation. In 1951 the community moved to Mount Abu and soon afterwards established centres in Delhi and Bombay. By 1969, when Lekhraj died, there were over 400 centres throughout India. Two women from the founding group, Dadi Prakashmani and Didi Man Mohini, then took responsibility for administration and the group moved into a new phase of expansion. In 1971 the first centres outside India were established in London and Hong Kong. By the early 1980s the movement was operating in over 40 countries. Following Didi Man Mohini's death in 1983, her place as joint head of administration was taken by Dadi Janki, another woman from the founding group. There are currently about 3,000 Brahma Kumaris centres in some 62 countries throughout the world. Each centre is normally guided by at least three Sisters who offer courses in meditation and in spiritual and moral values.

BKWSU is unique among Hindu religious organisations in being led by women. The Sisters receive fourteen years of training, in order to bring forth the loving qualities of *shakti – the female Hindu deity of Power – to the world. Purity and celibacy are emphasised. The group is vegetarian.

The Brahma Kumaris believe that – through the visionary experi-ence of their founder – *shiva has communicated to them the message that the world is approaching the end of the present historical era, which is known as the kali-yuga (literally 'Age of Kali'). Kali is the Hindu god-dess who, even more than *shiva, is associated with destruction. She is also seen as a life-giving mother. The Age of Kali has to be understood within the context of the doctrine of cosmic cycles that has for centuries been common both to Hinduism and Buddhism. It refers to the lowest phase in the cycle. It is seen as a dark age, an age of degeneration of human society, particularly in its spiritual and moral values and is 'characterised by strife, discord, quarrelling and contention; at the end of this age the world is to be destroyed'.[4] In keeping with Indian tradition the ending of the Age of Kali has been conceived by some members of the Brahma Kumaris as coming to pass violently, possibly as a result of nuclear war.[5] However, the good news is that a Golden Age, in which BKWSU will play a leading role – will begin after the end of the Age of Kali.

RAJA YOGA MEDITATION

Raja yoga meditation holds a central place in the life and work of the Brahma Kumaris. An introduction to meditation is given by the Brahma Kumaris as part of their public seminars on stress management. A typical setting for one of these would be a hotel conference room which has been carefully prepared to create the right atmosphere – subdued lighting, neatly-ordered chairs and soft music – designed to create a relaxed, quiet atmosphere. Those attending tend to be educated and middle-class for the most part, between the ages of 25 and 50, among them a fair sprinkling of those already involved in the practice of raja yoga.

Raja yoga meditation does not involve the use of mantras. In addition, little emphasis is given to hatha yoga postures or breathing exercises, both of which in germ at least are key elements of Patanjali's yoga. Instead, BKWSU stresses the importance of the mind and its powers. Nevertheless beginners are usually invited to prepare for meditation by using 'progressive muscular relaxation'.[6] This involves sitting with back upright and first becoming aware of, then moving, and finally relaxing, different parts of the body – toes, soles of the feet, calves, thighs, buttocks, back, arms, shoulders, neck and head. One is then invited to keep one's attention in the head and to 'relax the muscles of your mind'.[7] At this point one begins raja yoga meditation proper, which is performed with the eyes kept open throughout.

The first step in raja yoga meditation is to withdraw one's attention from the outside world and from one's body, focusing on the space at the centre of the forehead. This space is technically known as the *ajna* *cakra* ('command centre'), but popularly called the 'third eye'. This *cakra* is the one that is particularly active when the mind is at work. Keeping one's awareness on the *ajna *cakra*, one begins to direct one's thoughts in a positive way through visualisation and verbalisation. Typical of the phrases/thoughts which one might form in one's mind would be: 'I am peace ... Peace is my true state of being'; 'I now know my true self – an eternal, pure, peaceful soul'; 'I feel that everything is totally still – timeless'; 'I am with God in my eternal home of silence'; 'I absorb the Ocean of Peace'.[8] Along with phrases like these, one is encouraged to imagine situations such as a star or a point of light at the centre of the forehead, waves of peace washing over one, or an ocean of peace. Such images help to hold the attention on and give power to one's positive thoughts.

The effects of raja yoga meditation radiate from the *ajna *cakra* out into the meditator's body. Strong feelings of peacefulness, love and stillness can result. The meditator is encouraged to explore these associated feelings during meditation. One need only concentrate on the 'command centre' and in time the benefits of meditation will cascade down. As one raja yoga teacher put it: 'Once I get my higher values together, my lower values will take care of themselves'.[9] This is the reason why the Brahma Kumaris see no need to resort to the more earth-bound yogic techniques such as postures, breathing and use of mantras. However, there is a deeper reason why raja yogis do not concern themselves with physical yogic practices.

Raja yoga practice is based on the belief that human beings are essentially souls. The eternal soul is a person's true identity and meditation helps one to see both oneself and every other person 'as a soul'.[10] The body and the material world rank very low in this philosophy and are seen as the cause of all our ills. It is the soul that really matters. In a phrase that is reminiscent of Plato, raja yogis believe that 'The soul is like a driver and the body is the car'.[11] In order to be happy the only thing one need do is 'escape this physical world and fly to that timeless expanse, the soul world'.[12] The soul world is seen as a place of utter stillness, silence and peace. Happiness is guaranteed to those who manage to escape the physical world because 'in soul consciousness, the soul can only experience peace'.[13]

The Brahma Kumaris believe that the soul-consciousness that develops from meditation, helps one to see the good in others and to respect them. It will sustain a habit of acting altruistically in relation to other people. This is because one can give to others only what one possesses oneself and the raja yogin has the greatest gifts of all – clarity and strength of mind.[14] Soul-consciousness, together with the *sanskaras* – a Sanskrit term which will be looked at in the next paragraph – are seen as the keys to good ethical and social behaviour.

The Sanskrit word *sanskara* can probably best be translated as 'unconscious impression'.[15] The thinking behind the term is that each of our actions leaves a corresponding impression on the soul, of which the person is usually unaware. In the words of a BKWSU booklet, 'Habits, emotional tendencies, temperaments, personality traits are all built up by *sanskaras* imprinted on the soul'.[16] These personal characteristics in turn have an influence on how a person will think, judge and act in the future. BKWSU speaks of a three-phase cycle of first the 'mind' imagining and forming ideas; then the 'intellect' understanding and deciding around these ideas or images. In the third phase, the decisions of the intellect form and shape the *sanskaras*. The new *sanskaras* then feed back into the mind and the process starts all over again. It can readily be seen how a person can be caught in a bad cycle of thoughts and actions. However, beneficial intervention is possible through meditation, during which positive thoughts of peace can generate positive *sanskaras* and so create a good cycle. One can also create positive *sanskaras* by making positive choices within the intellect to change one's behaviour. Particularly effective is the mechanism known as 'giving'. Giving is the practice of 'having the thought to only spread peace and good wishes' – particularly applicable in situations where a relationship is hostile or uncomfortable.[17] The giver is amply rewarded in accordance with the law of *karma* whereby 'What I give out to the world and other people, I get back an equal amount'.[18]

In speaking about *karma* and the *sanskaras*, the booklet mentioned above makes no reference to any bodily life apart from the one that is being presently lived. In the context of the entire Hindu yogic tradition however, the law of *karma* and the *sanskaras* are viewed in the much wider context of all the other lives that one may have lived in the past or may yet live in the future. In this regard and in other ways raja yoga as practised by the Brahma Kumaris rests on the classical raja yoga of

Patanjali. The connection between the two will be studied next.

PATANJALI

According to Patanjali's philosophy reality is composed of two principles: *purusha*, which means 'spirit' or 'soul'; and *prakriti* or 'nature'.
Prakriti includes the entire material universe and in addition feelings,
thoughts, the ego and personality – everything in fact that is not spirit.
The true Self of each human being is spirit or soul alone, though most
people go through life remaining ignorant of this truth. Instead they
confuse spirit with the earth-bound psychological experience which is
known through the senses and the mind. And it is this confusion that is
the cause of all human suffering.[19] The soul from the moment of physical conception experiences itself as enmeshed in the material world, the
slave of ignorance of its own Self. In reality the Soul remains eternally
distinct from nature. It is only by escaping the 'illusion' that one is a
body-mind composite with its attachments and aversions, that one
awakens to one's true nature as an 'isolated, neutral, intelligent and inactive' soul.[20] The path to Self-realisation and freedom involves, on the
one hand, letting go of the false belief that one belongs to the realm of
prakriti; and, on the other hand, recognising one's true identity as a
soul or *purusha*. This Self-realisation automatically frees the 'enslaved'[21]
spirit. As a practical means of bringing this about, Patanjali described a
rigorous programme of yogic practice by which the soul strives to dis-
sociate itself from the material universe and so become free to 'enjoy' its
'natural' state of *kaivalya* ('isolation'). This programme consists of the
ashtanga ('eight limbs') described earlier.

Patanjali defines yoga as 'the restraint of the processes of the mind'.[22]
When this has been achieved, there will result 'the establishment of the
seer in his own nature', the 'seer' being the soul of the liberated yogi.[23]
Central to this process of liberation is the elimination of *sanskaras* or im-
pressions on the soul, because every *sanskara* is by definition an element of mental activity, which though dormant for the moment, must
inevitably give rise to further mental processes in the future. Patanjali's
yoga is a complex and finely-tuned discipline designed, not just to elim-
inate existing *sanskaras* but also, to ensure that the yogic practice itself

does not result in the formation of new ones.[24] The goal of the yogic quest is attained only as a result of strenuous ascetic effort over many lifetimes – the fruits of each lifetime being accumulated and passed on in the form of *sanskaras* to the next.

For Patanjali and the classical commentators on the *Yogasutras*, God (in Sanskrit *ishvara*) is not a creator nor does he intervene in human history. He is simply a special *purusha* who is distinguished from all others by the fact that he has been there through all eternity and has never been in bondage to the material principle *prakriti*. Though merciful, he helps people only in so far as each deserves.[25] Since every *purusha* is by nature inactive, *ishvara* inasmuch as he is a *purusha*, is incapable of actively helping people. The way in which *ishvara* can help has been compared to a magnet which, while itself remaining motionless nonetheless, causes movement in other bodies. *Ishvara's* presence alone is believed to remove obstacles in the way of people's performance of good deeds that will eventually over many lifetimes lead to liberation.[26] Here Mircea Eliade notes that later commentators on the *Yogasutras* tend to attribute a much larger role to *ishvara* than do the earlier commentators and Patanjali himself. This is because Hinduism had become much more mystical and devotional during the Indian medieval period as compared with Patanjali's time.[27]

As indicated above, Patanjali used the word *kaivalya* to describe the state of the completely liberated soul. Eliade translates *kaivalya* as 'absolute isolation'.[28] There is no longer any mere 'human' consciousness. Each individual liberated *purusha* or soul contemplates only itself. 'The cosmos is populated by these eternal, free, immobile purushas, monads among which no communication is possible ... this is a tragic and paradoxical conception of the spirit, which is thus cut off not only from the world of phenomena but also from other delivered "selves".'[29]

BRAHMA KUMARIS' THEOLOGY

The extent to which BKWSU has taken on the concept of *purusha* as applied both to human beings and to God is well summed up in a quotation from one of their leaflets: 'The human soul is recognised as a metaphysical, infinitesimal, eternal spark of sentient light. God is the Supreme among all souls with a form that is precisely the same – the infinitesimal spark of light. Human souls take on a physical body and mental energy is used to operate this vehicle for expression of thoughts, decisions and personality. God the Supreme is the one soul free from the limitations imposed by having a body'.[30] This statement approximates to a rather simplified summary of Patanjali's philosophy. However, the Brahma Kumaris' teaching has distinctive features of its own.

In contrast to the lonely destiny of the liberated as portrayed in the philosophy of Patanjali, those who faithfully practise raja yoga as taught by BKWSU are promised a personal relationship with God. Individual meditators can have a relationship with God not just after death, or after some highly advanced stage of yogic practice is attained, but quite early on during meditation. Meditation is seen as a meeting with God. As one focuses on the centre of the forehead and withdraws one's attention from one's surroundings and one's body, the meditator is invited to realise that he/she is 'with God in my eternal home of silence'.[31]

In the preceding section it was pointed out that the concept and role of God within the entire raja yoga tradition had become steadily more central in the centuries following Patanjali's time. For the Brahma Kumaris, the most significant development in this regard has been the experiences of the god *shiva which are believed to have been given to Dada Lekhraj. The same type of experience has been claimed a number of times over the intervening years by some of BKWSU's leaders. The visions of Lekhraj and his successors have affected the theology of BKWSU. Because of them, the God of the Brahma Kumaris seems nearer and more influential as compared with *ishvara in the raja yoga tradition generally.

BKWSU has an impressive record in terms of peace projects, building understanding between different religions, social and personal development and generally working towards a better world. Meditation is seen by the Brahma Kumaris as providing the motivation for action in the world. 'Raja Yoga meditation is not a rejection of the world, it is the preparation for life in the world. The detachment taught brings an objectivity that makes activity constantly positive'.[32] This statement could readily be adopted by Christians, who share the Brahma Kumaris' concern to make the world a better place. Christians however, unlike the

Brahma Kumaris, believe that the body and the material world, no less than the soul, are destined for salvation in Jesus Christ. This is quite the opposite to Patanjali and the classical raja yoga tradition in which detachment allows one to escape the world – a world of which the human person never really was part in the first place nor ever could be. In respectively affirming and denying the ultimate value of the material universe, Christians and classical raja yogis are each being consistent with their philosophies. The Brahma Kumaris however, seek to marry Patanjali's spirituality of disengagement with something that is not part of any traditional Hindu yoga: a mission to redeem the world. There is a dichotomy here. How can detachment which aims at enabling a person to 'escape this physical world' every time he or she sits down to meditate, also prepare one to become involved wholeheartedly and unselfishly in making that world a better place?[33] These counterflows within the heart of the Brahma Kumari are an enigma. What their possible effects may be on the lives of individual meditators – especially westerners – has yet to be fully investigated.

CAN YOGA BE CHRISTIAN?

The Christian response to the popularisation of yoga in the west has taken two forms. The first is represented in literature originating in some Protestant evangelical churches. Some of this sees no good at all in yoga. Yoga is viewed as highly dangerous: its practice is to be avoided at all costs.[1] More academic studies such as that of John Allan entitled *Yoga – a Christian Analysis*, examine different forms and schools of yoga, including several of those studied in the second part of this book.[2] Allan is dubious about the possibilities of using any yogic practices purely for improving one's health and he has considerable worries about possible occult or even demonic influences – 'at the very least the advanced yogi is leaving himself open to tremendous temptations'.[3] He does not encourage the view that some yogic techniques can be disengaged from their Hindu background and used to enhance the spiritual lives of Christians.

An alternative Christian response to the advent of yoga in the west and to yoga as encountered in its country of origin is more affirmative. This recognises in yoga approaches to spirituality that have the potential to contribute to a rejuvenated Christian spiritual praxis as well as an opportunity for dialogue with Hinduism. This approach has been spearheaded during the second half of the twentieth century by a small group of individuals mainly within the Roman Catholic tradition. These have opened up a range of possible uses for yoga within the context of Christian meditation and spirituality. Some leading figures in this process of dialogue between Christianity and Hinduism will be studied in some detail in the chapters that follow. Before this is done however, the question will be asked as to whether such an undertaking is permissible in terms of the Catholic Church's teaching.

THE RATZINGER DOCUMENT
In October 1989 the Congregation for the Doctrine of the Faith issued a 'Letter to the Bishops of the Catholic Church on some aspects of Christian Meditation'.[4] The letter was signed by Cardinal Ratzinger,

Prefect of the Congregation and it represents the Catholic Church's most authoritative statement to date on matters relevant to the application of yogic methods to Christian meditation.

Like the evangelical writers mentioned above, the Catholic Church too – going by the Ratzinger document – sounds a cautionary note where yogic practices are concerned. It stresses that 'getting closer to God is not based on any technique in the strict sense of the word', but is essentially God's gift.[5] It warns against identifying the grace of the Holy Spirit with any kind of psychological experience, or sensation of relaxation, light or warmth.[6] It holds that to regard these kinds of sensations as symbols of mystical experience 'when the moral condition of the person concerned does not correspond to such an experience, would represent a kind of mental schizophrenia which could also lead to psychic disturbance and, at times, to moral deviations'.[7] While the document does not make any specific reference to yoga apart from one footnote in the introductory chapter, it is true that psychological and sense experiences of the type referred to in the document are used widely within the yogic and particularly the *tantric* tradition as triggers for a variety of altered states of consciousness.

The Ratzinger document does not limit itself to issuing warnings about the dangers of meditation based on practices of non-Christian origin. On the positive side it states that ways of praying used by the great world religions should not be rejected out of hand simply because they are not Christian. It goes on to say that 'one can take from them what is useful so long as the Christian conception of prayer, its logic and requirements are never obscured'. It mentions with approval a number of specific practices from which Christians might receive inspiration, e.g., the 'humble acceptance of a master who is an expert in the life of prayer'.[8] This line can be understood to apply to – among others – the Hindu model of guru and disciple which is the traditional setting for yogic practice.

The document also makes the point that the emphasis placed on bodily posture, breathing and the heartbeat in the context of prayer, has for centuries been part of the spiritual traditions of Christianity – but those of the east rather than the west. Here physiological processes are utilised legitimately as symbols of spiritual experience – an example being the 'Jesus Prayer'. Despite the 'dangers' referred to above, the Ratzinger document acknowledges that genuine practices of meditation, not only from the Christian east, but also from the great non-Christian religions, can be 'a suitable means of helping the person who prays to come before God with an interior peace, even in the midst of external pressures'.[9]

At the time of its publication a number of Catholic commentators expressed disappointment at what they felt to be the negative tone of the Ratzinger document. However, bearing in mind that the role of the Congregation for the Doctrine of the Faith is that of 'goal-keeper' among the Church's departments, cautionary language was to be expected. Of much greater significance is that the Congregation left open the possibility for Christians to hold dialogue with non-Christians and, in the context of the present work, with Hindu yogis, hinging on the common experience (at least) of bodily posture and awareness, breathing and heartbeat.

PIONEERS IN THE DIALOGUE BETWEEN YOGA AND CHRISTIANITY

The spiritual leaders studied in the following chapters had done most of their work well before the Ratzinger document was published. Between them they incorporated a wide selection of yogic techniques into Christian spirituality. Contrary to what was suggested in some sections of the media at the time, Cardinal Ratzinger's letter in no way denigrated the theology of any one of them, or of others like them. On the contrary, it appeared to this writer to endorse – albeit cautiously – their general approach to using yogic techniques as means of becoming more open to union with God in Christ in a way that is faithful to the demands of Christian theology and spirituality.

JEAN DÉCHANET AND HATHA YOGA

Gabriel Déchanet was born in the Vosges region of France on 18 January 1906. On completing his secondary education, Déchanet decided to become a priest. However, he was unable to enter a seminary because he suffered from epilepsy and Church rules at that time forbade epileptics from receiving Holy Orders. Instead, he joined the Benedictine abbey of Saint-Andrè at Bruges in Belgium as a *familiaris* or lay member of the community. He received the habit in April 1925, taking the religious name of Jean-Marie.

In 1931 Jean-Marie read a book entitled *Letter to the Brothers of Mont Dieu* by the monk, theologian and mystic, William of Saint-Thierry. Over the following decades he was to become a world authority on Saint-Thierry, publishing some ten scholarly books plus numerous articles on him. He managed to combine his scholarship with service to the monastery which included taking care of the financial and practical needs of the abbey's missionary work in Africa.

As the result of a long period of treatment from a Bruges doctor, Déchanet was 'providentially cured' (as he put it) of his epilepsy. Now at the age of forty, he began to practise swimming and gymnastics. Noticing that physical exercise seemed to dispose him towards meditation, he began to practise yogic exercises. He was aware that these exercises went beyond the physiological level of postures and breath control – that they had a psychological and spiritual dimension. Through practising these yoga postures Déchanet found that his general health improved dramatically and his body became more supple. The monastic discipline of fasting, which he had previously found very difficult, became relatively easy. He found he was less susceptible to cold and less likely to develop a high temperature when he over-worked. He experienced a general sense of calm, and greater fidelity to his Christian calling and his religious vows. He became convinced that the ascetic discipline of yoga made it easier for the grace of Christ to flow in him.

Déchanet's improved health once again opened up for him the possibility of becoming a priest. After a period of preparation he was ordained in 1948.

In 1956 he published the first of his four books on yoga. It was entitled *La Voie du Silence*. Also in 1956 he went to the Belgian Congo (present-day Zaire) where for several years he was entrusted with the spiritual formation of African monks at the Kansénia mission in Katanga Province. Exhaustion and ill-health forced his return to Europe in 1964. He was given permission to live outside his monastery and he moved to Valjouffrey in the French Alps. There was one condition attached to this permission – he was not to do any work apart from leaving the door of his house open to whosoever might come to visit him. Over the years that followed many people were to come through this open door. Most of these were attempting to practise yoga in a Christian context and came to visit him for spiritual guidance. He continued with his writing, including the regular editing and publishing of a small magazine. During the summer months he held sessions in Christian yoga. In the wintertime his life was virtually that of a hermit.

With the passing years Déchanet's health became more precarious and the Alpine winter too severe for him. He returned to Bruges and Saint-Andrè in 1990. He died on 19 May 1992.[1]

Déchanet was, in his own words 'led to yoga by William of Saint-Thierry'.[2] The two strands of his intellectual life – medieval mystical theology and yoga – while superficially appearing to be unrelated, were intimately connected at a deep level. To better appreciate the connection, it is necessary to look briefly at the spirituality of Saint-Thierry.

BODY, MIND AND SPIRIT

William of Saint-Thierry (1085–1148) is named after the Benedictine Monastery of Saint-Thierry near Rheims, of which he was abbot. For much of his life he was a friend and supporter of Bernard of Clairvaux in the latter's work of establishing the new Cistercian Order of monks. William resigned his position of abbot of Saint-Thierry and left the Benedictine Order in 1135 to enter the newly-established Cistercian foundation of Signy. The remainder of his life there was dedicated to contemplation, study and writing.

Saint-Thierry taught that the human person functioned on three distinct levels. This view was uncommon among thinkers at that time. Traditionally, following the philosophies both of Plato and Aristotle, the human being was seen by most earlier Christian theologians as made up of two essential components: a physical body and a soul which by nature was designed to endure after bodily death. Some of the early Church fathers did however envisage a three-fold division of the human person into body, soul (or mind) and spirit.[3]

Saint-Thierry's three-dimensional picture of the human person profoundly develops the thinking of the fathers. It is also much more subtle than most contemporary uses of the body-mind-spirit terminology. He wrote in Latin and the terms which he used were *anima-animus-spiritus* which translate as 'animal soul' – 'rational soul' – 'spirit'. He understands these not simply as parts of a human being, but as dynamic principles or energies at work within the person. The animal soul or *anima* is that which gives life and purpose to the body and the senses; the *animus* or rational, thinking soul is the active mind which thinks and reflects on the world at large and on one's self. Each of these two principles represents ways in which the human being resembles God. The third principle, *spiritus* or spirit, goes beyond mere resemblance. Its function is to express our unity with God – *spiritus* is the level at which a relationship of love and mutual knowing between the human person and God takes place. With *spiritus* the human person is not so much acting, as being open to God's action. The Spirit of God at work within the human spirit brings about an experiential, loving knowledge, well-being and spiritual unity between the human being and God.

Saint-Thierry's three-fold division cannot be adduced from philosophy. For him it starts and ends with mystical experience. As Déchanet puts it, it is 'an attempt to express the inexpressible, by taking account of an empirical phenomenon perceived by all the saints – beyond the mind which thinks, reflects, elaborates on the gifts of the senses; beyond the intelligence itself which perceives and which knows after questioning and laborious examination, there is within the person a store of hidden energies, which are analogous to the powers of love'.[4]

The human person, according to Saint-Thierry, was made in the image of God but became separated from God by sin. Returning to God takes place progressively at the animal, rational and spiritual stages. However, this return is beyond the capacity of human nature to achieve of itself and can only come about as a result of God's gift.[5]

For many years before getting involved with yoga, Déchanet had made the spirituality of William of Saint-Thierry his own. On beginning his yogic practice he would have sensed a parallel between yoga and Saint-Thierry. The spirituality of Saint-Thierry does not 'separate the most exalted theory from what we contemporaries call "practice", from that which is at least accessible to us all. For him *theoria* and *praxis* are attracted to one another and interpenetrate'.[6] This interpenetration or at least non-separation of theory and praxis is also a defining characteristic of all forms of yoga. What he discovered within the yogic tradition were practical methods for training his body and mind to play their proper role in the 'return'. On beginning his yogic practice Déchanet was able to define his objective as to 'live entirely for God, to move towards him, with my "three" properly in balance, with my body playing its part, and my soul with all its lofty considerations withdrawing when required, so that the voice of the Almighty might be heard in my heart ...'[7]

CHRISTIAN YOGA

In the now classic book *La Voie du Silence* published in French in 1956, Déchanet introduced the term *'yoga chretien'*. The English edition published in 1960 highlighted this term through its title, *Christian Yoga*. Not all writers in east-west spirituality were happy with the term 'Christian Yoga' – notably Déchanet's Benedictine confrere, Henri Le Saux, better known by his Indian name, Abhishiktananda. He denied that there could be any such thing as a specifically 'Christian' yoga. In making this point he drew a parallel between yoga and such non-denominational disciplines as gymnastics or logic, saying: 'There is no such thing as a specifically "Christian" yoga, any more than there is Christian logic or Christian gymnastics.'[8]

Déchanet was well aware that yogic discipline had been developed within Hindu culture with the spiritual objective of reaching towards the Absolute Self. He determined to avoid this focus in his own practice saying: 'It was essential that my exercises and especially my concentration should turn me not towards the Self, the It, the Absolute, the Wholly-One, the vague "Ungraspable" of Hindu mystics, but towards the God of Abraham, Isaac and Jacob, the living God, three in one, the principle of all things, my Creator and Father, him in whom I had natural and supernatural life'.[9]

Before using the physiological and psychological practices of yoga to develop his approach to Christian spirituality, Déchanet planned to disengage them from their Hindu background and give them a Christian orientation. This applied particularly to the physical and relaxation exercises that are the usual starting point of yogic practice.

CHRISTIANISING HATHA YOGA

At the time when Déchanet was writing, hatha yoga was mainly presented to westerners as simply a system of physical self-development designed to promote bodily health and beauty. He recognised that, practised in that way, hatha yogic postures and breathing can lead to psychosomatic well-being, as he himself had discovered. However, he reminds us that in India yogic body exercise has always been a way of overcoming physical impediments that stand in the way of other, more spiritual, forms of yoga such as raja yoga. The true aim of all Hindu yoga is to bring about coherence amongst the various forms of vital energy and so assist a person 'to know and experience his true self and, in his true self, God'.[10]

Déchanet decided not to get involved at all with raja yoga and seemed to characterise it somewhat disparagingly as 'an absolute turning in on oneself; a condition where one has cut oneself off from everything, including all positive and objective knowledge'.[11] He understood raja yoga to involve practices such as mastering the circulation of the blood, and controlling the breath for hours on end along with protracted concentration. He did not feel himself ready to undertake the integration of these disciplines into Christian spirituality. Consequently he limited his agenda purely to basic hatha yoga practices, by which he meant yogic postures, breathing, and body awareness.

The first thing he had to do was to sort out theory from practice, and remove the hatha yoga exercises from 'the Brahmanic atmosphere that seems to be their matrix', before attempting to use them in a Christian context. Hindu teachings that needed particular attention here included the notion of the material world as a 'great illusion', and the spiritual goal of 'sublime isolation where the self claims to do without all help from on high'.[12]

Déchanet believed that a person's spiritual life could be enhanced by exercises in which body and soul are in possession of each other and work peacefully together. Thus, for him it is entirely proper to link physical exercises, postures and breath control with one's quest to grow in relationship with God. Here one is aiming to train and position the body in such a way that one becomes more open to the touch of God's Spirit. For example, when praying, one can take up one of the classical eastern meditation postures which are well known for promoting concentration of the spirit and inner recollectedness. Déchanet stresses that in recommending these practices he is not trying to 'compel the supernatural'.[13] The idea is simply to create an atmosphere of calm, peace and silence or harmony between body, soul and spirit so that nothing will hinder the work of grace.

EXERCISES

Déchanet's most popular works – *Christian Yoga* and in particular *Yoga in Ten Lessons* – are highly practical. Sections of these books bear a superficial resemblance to the vast 'yoga for health' literature in their illustrated descriptions of selections of postures deemed suitable for the westerner. However, Déchanet's choice of positions was governed by the 'primarily spiritual aims' of his books. He writes: 'Our whole aim is to bring calm and peace to the whole being; to make a good and faithful servant of the body; to free the soul from anxieties and problems that are, alas, all too common; and finally, to arouse the spirit'.[14] His schema of thirteen basic postures alternates between easy ones such as the 'Corpse' and the 'Forward Bend' and those that are relatively difficult such as the 'Plough' and the 'Headstand'.

From his own experience he verified that following a balanced programme of yogic exercise and relaxation produces many benefits. One of these is to facilitate the practice of the classical 'abstinences' (*yamas*) and 'disciplines' (*niyamas*) listed by Patanjali. The discipline of hatha yoga makes it easier for a person to live the principles of non-violence, simplicity, contentedness, truth, chastity, moderation and devotion to a personal God.[15]

Pranayama or yogic breath-control was likewise understood by Déchanet as being good both for one's health and one's life of prayer. The techniques he uses are drawn from the general hatha yoga tradition. They include the practice of alternate nostril breathing and 'squared' breathing, in which the same amount of time is given to each of the four phases of breathing: inhaling, holding the breath, exhaling and holding the lungs empty. A more advanced technique involves measuring the duration of inhalation, hold and exhalation to a count of three, twelve and six respectively (or four, sixteen and eight, etc.).

Another fundamental body rhythm which Déchanet incorporates into his programme is that of the heartbeat or pulsebeat. Awareness of this rhythm at various points in the body is used to relax deeply and to store energy. Alternately one can match the heartbeat to the rhythm of one's breathing.

All of the above exercises need to be situated within a life-style that is well-balanced and self-controlled. Déchanet recommends abstinence from strong liquor, tobacco and what he calls 'useless foodstuffs' among which he includes mushrooms and all condiments. Red meat is to be eaten sparingly. Regular fasting is recommended.

In all of the above Déchanet's focus reaches beyond the level of physical well-being, into the spiritual. Rhythmic breathing in particular he considered a great help in preventing the mind from being distracted during meditation. He believed that the gestures of those yoga practitioners who are involved in liturgy and monastic choral prayer would become much more expressive of the spiritual life that is within them. He especially recommended this kind of discipline for priests.

CHRISTIAN YOGA MEDITATION

Meditation – for Déchanet as for the Hindus – is at the core of yogic practice. And it is here that the key to Déchanet's thinking on yoga lies.

In speaking about a 'Christian Yoga', he means the use of techniques more usually found in the Hindu tradition to prepare the meditator for Christian contemplation. The object of meditation for the Hindu is, he tells us, 'the nature and essence of his true self'; whereas for the Christian the object of his meditation will be the God of Revelation. And yet, he insists, both can make use of the same techniques. This is because, in attempting to live spiritually, they start from the same human nature and as such have to overcome similar obstacles and difficulties.[16]

To begin meditation, he tells us, it is first necessary to sit still in one of the classical yogic seating postures. This will require considerable practice over a period of time. It will even involve a certain amount of suffering in which he sees a certain advantage. The bruising of the joints can be made to serve as 'a springboard for the spirit' particularly for someone striving to live the Christian life.[17] However, a new phase begins when the body becomes supple and the joints stopped complaining. From then on, the meditator finds himself spontaneously and gently drawn into silent meditation.

At the earlier stages of meditation Déchanet recommends the use of a short invocation either to the rhythm of the breath or the heartbeat. The second stage may be a period of silent 'gazing' on some object – for example, a candle flame, a simple religious image, a point in the body just above the heart or a mental image of Jesus drawn from Scripture or the Church's liturgy.

Apart from using sitting postures for meditation, Déchanet draws on the symbolic meaning of a number of other yogic postures to develop a body language for prayer. One of these, the posture he refers to as 'the Deep Obeisance', is more usually known as the 'Forward Bend' (padahastasana). He writes: 'As I bend forward for the Deep Obeisance I say "Our Father", and as I stand up again, "Thy Kingdom come"' – and (he tells us) there are other word combinations for this posture. The posture known as 'the Tree' (vrkshasana) likewise can be used to express many different prayers, for instance: 'All my heart goes out to thee, O Lord my God' or 'To thee, my God, do I lift up my soul'. With practice a point will be reached where the yogi will not need to find words to go with these movements. He will be able to express the feelings in his heart directly through these and other gestures.[18]

The fundamental rhythms of the body can also be used as foundations for prayer. While remaining attentive to the heartbeat one can form a repetitive prayer for each beat. Examples of this are 'My God' and the name 'Jesus'.[19] Even simpler is matching a prayer to the breath, for example, the words of Psalm 95 'Would you not listen to his voice today!' as one inhales; and 'Do not harden your hearts' as one exhales.[20]

In keeping with the best and most authentic traditions within both Hinduism and Christianity, Déchanet finally urges practitioners not to look for extraordinary sensations or psychological experiences.

THE LIMITS OF DÉCHANET'S APPROACH

In terms of the practices of yogic postures and breath control, Déchanet was self-taught. His knowledge of yoga was built up from his own study and practice. He did not have the opportunity to receive direct tuition in an Indian yoga ashram. Yoga schools in Europe were much more limited in the late 1940s and 1950s as regards both their numbers and the extent of their knowledge than has been the case in more recent decades. He is inaccurate in one or two physical details. Having correctly stated that men breathe naturally first through the abdomen and then through the chest, he goes on to say that women, when breathing naturally, begin the movement of inhalation with the chest and then through the abdomen.[21] It is generally accepted by yoga teachers today that the natural, relaxed 'full yogic' breath begins – for women as well as men – at the abdomen. The robust 'do it yourself' approach advocated by Déchanet is not favoured by most of those involved in teaching yogic practices to westerners nowadays. Teachers in India as well as in the west advise particular caution in regard to *pranayama*.

Déchanet's concerns are primarily with the lives of religious and priests, and with how to save the Church's liturgy from being merely external and help it become more prayerful. In adapting yoga techniques to Christianity, Déchanet worked within a very definite perspective. The context within which he wrote was the monastic routine which he lived. This is reflected in his thought patterns and vocabulary.

Most of Déchanet's writing was done before the Second Vatican Council and its changed vision of the relationship between the Roman

Catholic Church and non-Christian religions. It is thus hardly surprising that he takes for granted the superiority of the Christian mystical path compared with that of the 'Brahmanic, Buddhistic, Sufi and similar'.[22] In speaking of the Sanskrit term *samadhi* for example, he implies that it is a form of auto-suggestion and that it cannot be compared with the mystical experiences of Christian saints such as Catherine of Siena or Francis of Assisi. However, it would be unfair to judge the value of Déchanet's work on the basis of his pre-Conciliar views on the relationship between Christianity and other world religions. His basic approach to yoga and Christian spirituality is, like yoga itself, a practical one. The value of his 'Christian Yoga' must therefore be judged on its results. Even at the time of publication of his book of that name, encouraging testimonies as to its value were already to hand. Many more have since been added.

JOHN MAIN AND THE MANTRA

Fr John Main was born in London of Irish parents in 1926. He left school in 1942, working first as a journalist before taking up a post in radio and intelligence work with the British armed forces in war-time Belgium and Germany. After the war he joined the Canons Regular of the Lateran but left after four years. He then went on to study Law at Trinity College, Dublin, graduating in 1954.

Upon leaving College, Main accepted a position with the British colonial service in Malaya. While he was there he had a remarkable meeting that was to be the seed for the practice of meditation that would so profoundly mark the later course of his life. Years later Main described this encounter: 'I was first introduced to meditation long before I became a monk, when I was serving in the British colonial service in Malaya. My teacher was an Indian swami who had a temple just outside Kuala Lumpur'.[1]

The teacher in question was Swami Satyananda (1910–1961). He had travelled from Malaya to India to become a Hindu monk, inspired by figures such as Ramana Maharshi and Sri Aurobindo. Back in Kuala Lumpur Satyananda had founded the Pure Life Society in 1949, which in addition to spirituality, offered a variety of services, including courses in adult education. It also ran an orphanage and a library. The Swami agreed to teach Main how to meditate explaining: 'We use a "word" that we call a "mantra". To meditate, what you must do is to choose this word and then repeat it, faithfully, lovingly and continually'.[2] Except for one short interlude, John Main was to remain faithful to the daily practice of mantra meditation for the rest of his life.

Main left Malaya in 1956 and took up a post as lecturer in Law at Trinity College, Dublin. His promising career there was to last only three years. During this time he considered marriage but in September 1959 he joined the Benedictine Abbey in Ealing, London. After a one-year Novitiate he studied theology at the Benedictine College of Saint Anselmo in Rome. He was ordained priest in 1963 and soon after took up a position in the Abbey school at Ealing.

Six years later John Main was sent to the United States to the Catholic University in Washington. He had studied for less than a year when he was called to take over as headmaster of a Benedictine school just outside Washington. In 1974 he was recalled to Ealing. John Main's real mission would now begin.

Behind the busy life of scholar and teacher, John Main had all along been seeking some way of validating his own spiritual practice as learned from Swami Satyananda. His own meditation had provided an anchor for his life both in Malaya and back in Dublin. It had in a sense led him to the monastery gate and sustained his life as a monk. He now wanted above all to know if this form of meditation could be offered as an authentic form of Christian prayer, whether he might legitimately pass on to others what he himself had learned and practised.

In the *Conferences* of the fourth-century desert monk John Cassian, Main believed that he had discovered a Christian source for the image-less mantra prayer that he had learned from Swami Satyananda. He now felt able to reconcile his experience of eastern meditation with the Christian monastic tradition. Soon he began to teach his own distinctive form of Christian meditation. The first step was the establishment early in 1975 of a lay community comprising four young men who had come to learn how to meditate. Side by side with this community, the first of many Christian meditation groups – people coming to meditate together once a week – began to develop.

In July 1975 John Main was narrowly defeated in the election for Abbot of Ealing. Instead he was appointed prior and novice master. As the Abbey at that time had only one novice – Brother Laurence Freeman – Main spent much of the following year on the road, giving retreats and lectures on Christian meditation. He soon became convinced that the traditional monastic setting was no longer the place from which to continue his mission of teaching meditation. So in September 1977, accompanied by Laurence Freeman, he travelled to Montreal to establish a community wholly dedicated to the practice of Christian meditation. In a house which they purchased with the generous assistance of the local bishop, the beginnings of a monastic programme of Divine Office, Eucharist and daily work began to take shape. From the outset the Benedictine Priory of Montreal was known as a centre to which all were welcome to come and meditate. In less than a year there was a meditating community of resident and non-resident monks, sisters, lay people and families.

The practice of Christian meditation as taught by John Main was at this time becoming more and more widespread not just in Canada, Britain and Ireland, but in many other parts of the world. This was happening through Main's writings and cassette tapes, as well as lecture tours and retreats conducted by himself and later by Laurence Freeman who was ordained a priest in 1980. With John Main's encouragement and under his direction an international network of meditation groups began to form and grow.

Early in 1982 John Main was diagnosed with secondary cancer of the lungs. He had previously recovered from a cancerous colon, but this second illness was inoperable. He hid it from all but a few of his closest friends and carried on with his work. In the summer he travelled to Britain and Ireland to lecture and to say goodbye to his family. Back in the Montreal Priory Main continued to celebrate the Eucharist and give his regular talks on meditation from a wheel-chair. He died in December 1982.

John Main's vision and life's work continues under the direction of his disciple and successor, Laurence Freeman. Although the priory in Montreal closed in 1990, the numbers of people using the John Main approach to Christian meditation, continues to grow. There are groups of meditators right across North America, Europe, Asia, Australia and more recently in some African countries.

HOW TO MEDITATE

More than a dozen books and a whole library of cassette tapes of talks by John Main himself and his successor Laurence Freeman are now in print. These short talks were originally given as introductions to meditation sessions in the Montreal Priory and elsewhere. The tapes have since been widely used for the same purpose by meditation groups throughout the world. These books and tapes are mainly inspirational in character. They are rich in practical theology and in references to Scripture and the whole corpus of Christian literature. In particular they deal with the psychology of the meditator as he faces into the demands which a serious programme of meditation will make of him.

The essence of the John Main approach to meditation is expressed very simply at the beginning of several of the books:

'Sit down. Sit still and upright. Close your eyes lightly. Sit relaxed but alert. Silently, interiorly begin to say a single word. We recommend the prayer-phrase "maranatha". Recite it as four syllables of equal length. Listen to it as you say it, gently but continuously. Do not think or imagine anything – spiritual or otherwise. If thoughts and images come, these are distractions at the time of meditation, so keep returning to simply saying the word. Meditate each morning and evening for between twenty and thirty minutes.'[3]

The mantra *maranatha* is an Aramaic word which is rooted in the New Testament (II Cor 16.22, Rev 22.2) and other early Christian literature. Its meaning is uncertain. It can be read as *maran atha* ('the Lord has come') or as *marana tha* ('our Lord, come!'). Recited as four syllables: *ma-ra-na-tha*, it has an even, mantric quality.

Main did not insist that this mantra only be used and many who follow his way of prayer do so with other mantras – sometimes non-Christian ones. As an example of this, he was content to allow some meditators who had previously been practising Transcendental Meditation to continue using their TM mantra.[4] This was an acknowledgement of the difficulty of changing a mantra that had become deeply rooted. It also served to underline Main's belief that it is not the mantra that makes meditation Christian, but a context of faith and love within the Christian meditating community. He did however stress that, after a period of experimentation, one should decide on and persevere with one mantra. This is because the poverty of a single word is an essential ingredient of the discipline of Christian meditation.

A crucial element in the discipline of meditation is the amount of time that one commits to it. The minimum requirement of twenty minutes each morning and evening is reminiscent of Transcendental Meditation and as in the case of TM is designed to help the mantra become rooted in the mind and heart. This similarity probably stems from the fact that both TM and John Main's meditation share a common background within the Hindu tradition of *japa or mantra recitation.

John Main's teacher, Swami Satyananda was influenced by Ramana
Maharshi (1879–1950), the great sage of Arunachala in south India who
also inspired Abhishiktananda. Ramana was a *jnana yogi or one who
practised the 'yoga of knowledge' in the context of the *vedanta *advaita
philosophy. The object of this form of yoga is to 'dive' within oneself in
order to experience 'Self-realisation' which is identical with the state of
*advaita or the experience of oneself as not different from *brahman, the
one and only Reality.[5]

For Ramana the great barrier on the road to Self-realisation is the
ego which is the source of all our thoughts.[6] One will never be free from
thoughts until the ego is crushed.[7] Only then can the mind become 'one-
pointed' or quiescent. One of the instruments recommended by him to
achieve this is the repetition of mantras.[8] *Japa or mantra recitation
'means clinging to one thought to the exclusion of all other thoughts'.[9]
However, the purpose of meditation is to strengthen the mind to the
point where it can be free of all thoughts.[10] In time one may be brought
to a condition that is beyond words and thoughts: that is, *advaita.[11]

In his theology John Main drew a parallel between the Hindu *advaita doctrine and the way the Christian meditator stands in relation to
God. In one of his letters he wrote: 'There is the true self (*atman) which
is Christ. In him, with him and through him we are in God (*brahman).
There is the false self (Ego) which has no reality and does not exist – it
is only an illusion. The false self burns away and gives way to the true
self in the fire of Divine Love who is Christ'.[12]

Mantra recitation as taught by John Main has some similarity with
mantra recitation in the *advaita tradition in that it is designed to bring
the meditator beyond words, thoughts, images and the false self or ego.
The reason for reciting the mantra from beginning to end of the meditation does not stem from a belief that the mantra has power of itself to
achieve anything. Rather is it a discipline to turn away from the ego. As
the meditator seeks to focus his whole attention on the mantra, his consciousness will be assailed by an endless series of distracting thoughts
and images. The appropriate way of dealing with these distractions is
'returning to simply saying the word'. This will constitute a sacrifice of
something we hold very dear – our own ideas and familiar images. In

a very real sense the meditator lays down his life – his false self. The meditator is thus practising detachment every time he re-focuses his attention on the mantra and away from an attractive idea or image. Over time this will build up a spirit of detachment in the meditator. As in the case of Ramana's meditation it quietens the mind and leads one to a deeper state of awareness.[13]

While the practical aspects and the psychology of meditation as taught by John Main and the Hindu tradition are analogous in some respects, they differ in regard to what meditation is aiming at. For Ramana Maharshi and the *advaita *vedanta tradition generally, the condition to be aimed at is the realisation at an intuitive – not a rational – level that 'the Self is all'.[14] To say 'the Self is all' is to assert that the deep Self of the meditator is nothing other than *atman, the Self or Soul of the world, which in turn is not different from *brahman, the ultimate principle of all existence. John Main on the other hand interprets the experience of mantra meditation in terms of Christian scripture and spiritual traditions.

CHRISTIAN MEDITATION

John Main's vision of the dynamic at work in Christian meditation builds on the detachment which is the fruit of faithful perseverance in the recitation of one's mantra. Starting and continuing the repetition of the mantra from the beginning to the end of each meditation builds patience and in time leads to greater freedom, particularly in regard to one's ideas. The resulting openness of mind leaves the meditator more disposed to practising the two fundamental commandments of Christ – love of God and love of one's neighbour. This as taught in the Gospel leads to eternal life. Schematically this can be represented as 1 – detachment, 2 – freedom, 3 – love, 4 – fullness of life.[15]

Initially the practice of meditation tends to produce a feeling of relaxation and mental well-being. Those who persevere in the Main approach to meditation will soon realise how difficult it is to keep their attention on the mantra or even to continue reciting or sounding the mantra for the duration of the time spent at meditation. This leaves one with a sense of disappointment in oneself. In the words of one meditator: 'At the end of most sessions all I had to offer the Lord was my failure to do something so simple as to stay with the mantra. Of course, the alternative might have been to be able to offer fantastic insights into the meaning of a gospel passage or exciting feelings of fervour about some scene, or deep remorse about the past or great plans for the future ... But to offer failure, nothing, is really to leave self behind and follow Him'.[16] The Christian meditator is asked to experience pain, privation and death during his meditation – as indeed will oftentimes happen in his life as well.

Christian meditation is thus a microcosm of the Christian life as a whole inasmuch as it involves processes of letting go and dying – just as Christ himself surrendered to death on the Cross and subsequently experienced his Resurrection. This assimilation of the meditator to Christ both in his dying and in his rising is no mere metaphor but is at the heart of traditional Christian theology and spirituality. In the words of St Paul: 'If we have died with him we shall also live with him' (II Tim. 2.11). Theologians have articulated Scriptures like this as the doctrine of the Divine Indwelling, the teaching that the risen Jesus really dwells in the heart of the believer.[17] According to this theology, which John Main followed, the only real Christian prayer is the prayer of Christ in the heart of his disciple. By keeping one's attention on the mantra as it is repeated, the meditator – according to John Main's spirituality – leaves himself open to being taken over by the Spirit of Jesus and so becoming a participant in the universal prayer of Jesus to the Father.

In practice the experience of resurrection is not always evident during the individual meditation session, which can sometimes be a painful turning away from one distraction after another. However, after some weeks or months of the practice, certain changes may become evident in the meditator and perhaps more to those who live close to her than to herself. The person may be less prone to angry outbursts, less controlling of others' lives, more generous in sharing her possessions and time with others or more willing to face the truth about herself. This is far more of an acid test of the Christian dimension of a meditative experience than is the peaceful, relaxed feeling that soon results from most approaches to meditation. In Gospel terms the Christian meditator is challenged to experience the Cross of Jesus in order to live in the life of the Resurrection. Laurence Freeman numbers among those who are sustained by Christian meditation in the John Main tradition: volunteers in refugee camps, unemployed people, a wealthy couple who put their house at the service of exhausted missionaries, recovering alcoholics, l'Arche workers, parents and children, politicians, priests and religious.[18]

MEDITATION AND THE CHRISTIAN COMMUNITY

Not surprisingly, some people have questioned whether the very simple, almost stark form of mantra meditation espoused by John Main is in tune with the age old tradition of Christian prayer. Ambrose Tinsley, OSB, knew John Main and on occasion has sat down to meditate with him. He compared Main's approach with another mantra-like form of Christian meditation, the Jesus Prayer. He considered that the latter 'seemed to have a warmth and an attractiveness not found in his (Main's) somewhat austere demands'.[19] Tinsley would prefer a form of prayer that allowed more space for the affective side of the human person and greater flexibility generally: '... within the group itself instead of the imperative, "repeat your mantra" it is often better only to suggest that if a word emerges to express one's personal response to God one should allow it to repeat itself'.[20]

A particular question that has been raised is whether Main's imageless prayer is suited to those whose knowledge of and commitment to the Christian life are as yet little developed. In this context reference is made by both John Main's supporters and his critics to the fourteenth century spiritual classic *The Cloud of Unknowing* – but with differing interpretations. In his prologue the author of this work emphasises that it is not even to be read by those who are not 'wholly determined to follow Christ perfectly'. Writing on behalf of the John Main tradition, Laurence Freeman considers this warning to be a 'historical conditioning'.[21] John Grennan, ODC, who lectures in spirituality, disagrees with this interpretation and stresses the importance of always 'keeping one's life consistent with one's prayer'.[22] Meditation that is not linked to a serious effort to live the Christian life faithfully can, he warns, even be counter productive: 'a danger of adopting a contemplative technique before the time is right is that it simply locks one further into the world of selfishness; the activity that passes for contemplative prayer becomes a resting place in oneself rather than a transcendent outreach to God'.[23]

This discussion serves to focus attention on the context within which meditation takes place. And here it must be acknowledged that John Main – unlike much of the Hindu tradition from which he learnt so much – taught that meditation should be a means of building and renewing community. Contemplative experience 'should not, as so often in the east, be narrowly restricted to the state of solitude and withdrawal from the world'.[24] The practice of Christian meditation as used by John Main has in fact been spread mainly as a result of groups of people sitting down together to meditate – usually on a weekly basis. In some instances the element of community interaction has been taken much further. Gerry Pierse, CSSR, wrote a report on his experience with a group of Filipino parishioners. These came together once a week to share their personal reflections of pre-selected passages of Scripture. After some months the group took up twice-daily meditation in the tradition of John Main. For many there was an initial period of euphoria. This was followed by a 'dry' period of tenaciously continuing the mantra, during which the support of the group was a clear help. The fruits then began to appear in the form of a growing concern for social justice, greater patience, remembrance and healing of long-forgotten hurts.[25] Pierse summarises the role of Christian meditation in relation to Christian living: 'The total poverty of the silence of the mantra creates a hunger for scripture and the letting go of anything in one's life that is inconsistent with being in God's presence'.[26]

Anthony de Mello's
Sadhana

Anthony de Mello was born in Bombay in 1931. On completion of his schooling he joined the Bombay Province of the Society of Jesus. As a Jesuit, he was sent to study philosophy in Barcelona but returned to India to do his theology at De Nobili College in Poona. After his ordination to the priesthood there was additional overseas study – in Chicago and Rome where he studied psychology and spirituality respectively.

The early years of De Mello's ministry as a priest were spent in retreat work and spiritual direction mainly in India. This work gradually evolved into the Sadhana spirituality courses which he began in Poona. In 1978 he relocated the Sadhana programme to the town of Lonavla, which is situated between Poona and Bombay. 1978 was also the date of publication of his first book which was entitled *Sadhana – a Way to God*.

From 1978 onwards, De Mello's life was divided between writing, running courses – some as long as nine months – at Lonavla, and intense lecture tours in many countries, particularly in the United States. It was while on one of these tours that he died suddenly in New York in June 1987.

FROM SPIRITUAL DIRECTOR TO MEDITATION TEACHER

De Mello joined the Jesuits from a traditional Indian Catholic family. His Jesuit training was based first and foremost on the spirituality of Ignatius of Loyola, the society's founder. In time De Mello came to be recognised especially among religious and priests as a master in the use of the spiritual exercises of Saint Ignatius.

A volume of his retreat notes written in the earlier years of ministry but published only after his death shows De Mello as a brilliant though relatively conventional preacher of the 1960s and early 1970s.[1] Based on the Scriptures, this writing is mainly explanatory and exhortatory, but does reveal the occasional use of awareness and fantasy techniques which would flower in his later work.[2]

During the 1970s, De Mello developed the group meditations that were to become a central part of his Sadhana programme. These exercises would form the basis for two of his best known books – *Sadhana* and *Wellsprings*. A typical meditation as found in these works is structured as follows:[3]

A. Awareness of:

1) sensations within the body.

2) sounds round about.

3) one's own breathing.

B. Fantasy: this may be an imaginary situation involving oneself in a scene from nature or the Gospel. Frequently it includes a meeting with Jesus Christ.

C. Awareness of feelings that result from the fantasy.

D. Brief recapitulation of the awareness sequence in A.

Sadhana is divided into three sections entitled respectively 'Awareness', 'Fantasy' and 'Devotion'. Virtually every one of the 47 meditation exercises of which the book is comprised makes use of awareness and fantasy techniques. All of the 81 exercises in *Wellsprings* are fantasies. De Mello's psychological training was of great significance in his use of these techniques.

THE INFLUENCE OF JOHN O. STEVENS

As a result of his studies in the United States during the 1970s, De Mello was influenced by a variety of figures in the field of psychotherapy, particularly the Rogerian school. Among these were Carl Rogers himself and Eric Berne.[4] De Mello drew deeply from a book by a younger psychotherapist, John O. Stevens entitled *Awareness: exploring, experimenting, experiencing*.[5] This work is a comprehensive collection of some 200 exercises in various kinds of awareness. The approach is systematic and detailed. Stevens regards his work purely as therapy and he makes no attempt to give it a spiritual orientation. Stevens was a disciple of Fritz Perls (1893–1970) who is the father of Gestalt Therapy. Perls believed that 'awareness is the only basis of knowledge and communication' and that it is curative.[6]

De Mello cited the authority of Ignatius and in particular the practice known as 'composition of place' to justify his use of fantasy in the context of Christian prayer.[7] However, there is reason to believe that Steven's work supplied him with practical methods for doing this. There are many parallels between *Awareness: exploring, experimenting, experiencing* on the one had and De Mello's *Sadhana* and *Wellsprings* on the other. These include the use of awareness as a means to identify with one's present experience and the recognition that awareness of one's own body automatically leads to an easing of tightness and tension.[8] Both authors recognise the value of awareness exercises for leaving past and future aside, keeping one focused in the present tense, identifying fully with one's own experience and accepting the way one actually is instead of dwelling on the fantasy of how one wants to be.[9]

Some of the meditations in Steven's book have been imported unchanged into the De Mello tradition. An example of this is the one called 'Rosebush Identification'[10] which, though not described in any of De Mello's books, has been widely used in workshops on De Mello's spirituality.[11] The purpose of this and other identification exercises is as a means to self-knowledge and self-acceptance. The Symbolical Fantasy exercise in *Sadhana* in which one is invited to interact with a statue of oneself is evidently based on the Fantasy Journey 'Statue of yourself' in *Awareness*.[12]

There are sections in *Awareness* that have no equivalent in any of De Mello's books. These are the groups of exercises entitled 'Communicating with Others', 'Pairs', 'Couples' and 'Group Activities'. In De Mello's written works the emphasis is on the contemplative journey of the individual. However, in the workshops that he directed at Lonavla and elsewhere there was a considerable amount of working with groups of two or more people, using exercises from the above-mentioned groups.

AWARENESS AND CONTEMPLATION

For De Mello contemplation means communication with God that dispenses with or makes a minimum use of 'words, images and concepts'.[13] In this sense he holds that awareness can in itself be a form of contemplation. As he puts it: 'All the glory of a mountain sunrise and much, much more, is contained in so drab an exercise as being aware of your body sensations for hours and days on end'.[14] The practice of awareness helps in overcoming addictions and can lead to the development of such qualities as sincerity, simplicity, kindliness and patience.[15] It also leads to the revelation of one's self.[16] Some of De Mello's awareness exercises, particularly those dealing with body sensations, are no less detailed than Stevens'. To those who would practice them, however, he warns against the temptation to seek a trance state, rather like self-hypnosis. This has nothing to do either with the sharpening of awareness or with contemplation.[17] One also needs to be temperate in practising awareness of one's breathing. Otherwise, hallucinations may be produced.[18]

Apart from simple consciousness of one's breathing and one's body sensations, the practice of awareness covers a wide range of subjects. These include mental awareness – staying with one's stream of consciousness whilst thinking. Body awareness includes such practices as moving each part of one's body slowly and deliberately whilst walking, and using gesture as a body language for prayer. Awareness of sensation includes a method of coping with mild pain by focusing all of one's attention in detail on the area affected.

The deeper levels of contemplation in many spiritual traditions call for a psychological state beyond words, images and concepts. Here, De Mello cites the author of the *Cloud of Unknowing* and John of the Cross in his reference to the 'Dark Night of the Senses'. The challenge in prayer of this kind is to resist the temptation to start thinking and imagining and to be willing simply to sit in the dark, in the emptiness and 'gaze at the blank lovingly'.[19] In practice this might mean the silent repetition of a prayer word, gazing on a religious image, or simply being aware of one's breathing or body sensations.

A devotional dimension can readily be added to many awareness exercises. An example of this is in Exercise 14 of *Sadhana*.[20] First he takes the reader through a detailed awareness of a familiar object such as a pen or a cup using the senses of seeing, smell, touch and taste. He then extends the meditation with the words: 'Now place yourself and this object in the presence of Jesus Christ ... Listen to what he has to say to you and to the object ...' Awareness prepares the ground for fantasy, in this case a fantasy which is built within a Christian faith context.

The later sections of *Sadhana* and the whole of *Wellsprings* develops and expands in many directions the use of fantasy in Christian meditation.

FANTASY

The longest and most detailed as well as the greatest number of De Mello's meditations come under the heading of fantasy. All begin with some preliminary practice of awareness. From then on the fantasies themselves take a wide variety of forms. Several of the meditations have a world-wide cosmic aspect. In these he takes the meditator in fantasy thousands or even millions of years into the past or the future and invites him or her to gaze across an endless desert or the depths of space.[21] Such fantasies help one put one's own problems and concerns into perspective or, as he puts it: 'Solitude gives distance, Distance brings serenity ...'[22] Other exercises involve entering into dialogue with visualised archetypes such as 'the temple of a lost religion' or a wise holy man.[23]

De Mello borrows from diverse religious and secular traditions. One of the more powerful meditations is Exercise 29 of *Sadhana* entitled 'Fantasy on the corpse', which is of Buddhist origin. The reader is invited to vividly imagine his own corpse as it goes through nine different stages of decomposition. The purpose of this exercise is 'to offer you the gift of peace and joy and help you to live life in greater depth'.[24] For those who find this meditation unappealing, there is a range of slightly less graphic exercises which involve living in fantasy such things as blindness, paralysis, death and one's own funeral.[25] Difficult as these may appear, the experience of those who practise them has frequently been a sharper awareness and appreciation of some of God's greatest gifts – sight, movement, health and life itself. In general, De Mello's fantasies can help one to know and accept oneself at a deeper level. The fantasy on a statue of oneself referred to earlier is a case in point. Looking at, touching, speaking to and finally becoming one's own statue is for most people a self-revelation. Dialogues with the body,[26] a trip into the desert or into the heart of the unborn child,[27] journeys through the various stages of one's own life and death,[28] entering into challenging scenes of concentration camps, wars and famine,[29] or contrasts such as birth/death, wedding hall/cancer ward, sports stadium/old folks home, luxury hotel/slum:[30] all are designed to help one experience oneself in unexpected and enriching ways.

Themes from nature run through many of the exercises – and not only the obviously beautiful ones such as dawn, sunset, and flowers. The meditation in *Wellsprings* entitled 'The Kingdom'[31] dwells on nature's harsher edge: 'the seed that is sown only to perish', 'trillions of wasted eggs and foetuses destroyed', 'incapacitating sickness'. This kind of exercise finds its resolution only in failure, the unsuccessful mission of Christ – yet vindicated by his Resurrection.

De Mello wanted his work to be for persons of all spiritual affiliations and none. However, more often than not he adds a final step to facilitate those who would like to make the meditation an exercise specifically in Christian spirituality. Typically, he adds words like 'Christ was in that event. Where was he? Can you observe him acting in it? How does he act?'[32] In regard to the fantasy of oneself as a statue, he invites the meditator to imagine Jesus walking into the room, looking at and speaking to the statue.

Many of De Mello's meditations – particularly in *Wellsprings* – begin with a scene or text from the Christian scriptures. Most are in the form of Gospel fantasies in which the reader is invited to imagine the setting as vividly as possible, see people, participate in the action, take note of one's feelings and most importantly, relate in faith to Jesus. The influence of the Ignatian tradition in De Mello's work is evident in these exercises. It is of no importance that one's fantasy is not geographically accurate. De Mello makes the telling point that even though Ignatius had himself been to the Holy Land as a pilgrim and could have given accurate and detailed descriptions, nonetheless he 'invites the exercitant to invent his own Bethlehem, his own Nazareth, the road to Bethlehem, the cave where Christ was born, etc.'[33] The subjects of De Mello's Gospel meditations include the cure of a paralysed man at the pool of Bethzatha, the wedding feast of Cana and Jesus preaching in various parts of Galilee. One of the many fantasies on the Passion of Jesus – Exercise 20 in *Sadhana* – is developed as a method for coping with resentments.

The deeper aim of meditation is a contemplative silence. Fantasy and awareness exercises, De Mello reminds us, are simply means to that end. In the introduction to *Wellsprings*[34] he compares the book to 'a staircase to get up to the terrace. Once there, be sure to leave the stairs, or you will not see the sky. When you are brought to silence this book will be your enemy. Get rid of it'.

STORY

The human heart longs for truth and at the same time people's first reaction to truth tends to be fear and hostility. This mysterious fact is – according to De Mello – the reason why great religious teachers like Buddha and Jesus created stories as a way to get behind the opposition of their listeners. Through listening to and reflecting on an appropriate story well told, one can be drawn into accepting some truth about oneself that may lie hidden in the story – and hidden in one's own unconscious.[35]

De Mello's published collections of story-meditations comprise stories and anecdotes culled from the folklore of many lands: India, China, Russia and Europe.[36] Many of them are religious and come from all the main traditions: Hindu, Buddhist, Muslim, Jewish and Christian. De Mello himself seems to have been particularly partial to stories from the Zen Buddhist and Sufi traditions. By reading and reflecting on the anecdotes of each collection in the order in which they were written, the reader is led through the major themes of these books: the unknowability of God, prayer, true versus false religion, challenges to accept the uniqueness of each human person and the responsibility to live fully in the present moment of time. Many of the anecdotes selected by De Mello seem designed to disturb or even shock the reader into re-examining long-cherished religious beliefs. A number are in the form of riddles or jokes. The reader may be tempted to read quickly through these stories in order to be entertained or amused. If however, as De Mello urges, a person is prepared to dwell on a story, to reflect and carry it around within himself, it will begin to reveal unrecognised home truths. As he tells his readers: 'Every one of these stories is about you'. To illustrate how this process might work one can refer to a short anecdote that he gives in his introduction to *The Prayer of the Frog*: 'Excellent sermon,' said the parishioner, as she pumped the hand of the preacher.

'Everything you said applies to someone or other I know'.

Initially the reader smiles at the parishioner who sees the need for change in everyone but herself. However, on reflection the reader may wonder if he or she may not in reality have the same attitude towards personal change as that parishioner, i.e., it is others who need it! This is what one might term the second level of interaction between the story and the listener/reader. But there is a third level which not many have the patience to move on to. If someone is prepared to return to the story again and again and to spend time with it – meditating on it, carrying it around in one's mind – hidden aspects of oneself will be brought from unconsciousness to consciousness. The story will bring about change in one's life. The end result will be greater humility and openness. As De Mello puts it: 'The story will worm its way into your heart and break down barriers to the divine'.[37]

DE MELLO AND THE INDIAN TRADITION

The influence of Buddhism is explicit throughout De Mello's life and work. He attended at least one Buddhist retreat – probably under the direction of the renowned teacher S. N. Goenka.[38] Goenka is an ethnic Indian who grew up in Burma and was trained in the techniques of Vipassana meditation which are so strong in that country. Since the late 1960s he has been based in Poona, working as a master of the Vipassana tradition. His approach has been so well received that he currently presides over a network of meditation centres and teachers in more than a dozen countries.

In *Sadhana* De Mello gives some indication of how his practices of sitting for meditation and becoming aware of one's body sensations and breathing were influenced by his experience while on a Buddhist meditation retreat.[39] Reference has already been made to the 'Fantasy on the corpse', one of several exercises which are of Buddhist origin. As a final hint of his close contact with the Buddhist tradition, one of the last letters written by De Mello before his death was to the Buddhist teacher Achaan Chah.

Curiously, the term 'yoga' hardly occurs at all in De Mello's writings. However, in his work as a teacher of spirituality, he used practical methods which are little different from those used by the swamis of the Indian yogic tradition. These take a number of forms.

The exercises entitled 'Stillness' in *Sadhana* and 'The Arrival' in *Well-springs*[40] are simply a form of the classical *yoga nidra* or 'yogic sleep' as practised for instance in the contemporary school of Satyananda Swami. The practice of 'composition of place' as originally developed by St Ignatius has no connection with India. However, there are clear parallels between it and the practice of *pratyahara* or 'sense-withdrawal' which has been an active element in the yogic tradition since the time of Patanjali.[41] The listening exercises described under the heading 'Sounds' in *Sadhana* are evidently derived from an ancient yogic 'sound and light' tradition.[42]

The methods that De Mello uses in his spirituality relate most of all to the **tantric* and **jnana* traditions of yoga. These will now be looked at separately.

TANTRIC YOGA AND THE JESUS PRAYER

Some of De Mello's fantasy meditations involve allying the imagination with the physiological functions of sensing, hearing, breathing or movement. An example of this is found in Exercise 6 in *Sadhana* which is entitled 'God in my breath': '... Think of the air as of an immense ocean that surrounds you ... an ocean heavily coloured with God's presence and God's being ... While you draw the air into your lungs you are drawing God in ...'[43] In Exercise 10 he invites the reader to 'Feel God's power at work in the production of every single sensation'.[44] Exercise 9 shows how various bodily gestures, when carried out with consciousness of every movement, can become a body language for prayer expressing adoration, self-offering, surrender.[45] The practice of using a physiological function to embody a spiritual principle is widely used in the **tantric* yoga tradition. De Mello's spirituality shares with tantrism the aim of incarnating spirituality within the body and in everyday realities. Experiences of physical awareness are universal to all cultures. Since they take place in the body and not in the mind they are intellectually 'blind' and can therefore co-exist with almost any spiritual philosophy. The tantrists use awareness exercises with the aim of bringing about the integration of the individual self with the universal Self (*atman*).[46] De Mello's spiritual objective is a stronger sense of the presence and the power of God, specifically in the form of Jesus or the Holy Spirit. Many of his exercises have a *repertoire* of forerunners in the literature of the Hindu *tantras*.

There is one particular form of Christian prayer using physiological awareness that does not have any evident connection with the Hindu *tantric* tradition. This is the 'Jesus Prayer'. Though apparently dating from the earliest centuries of the Church's history, this prayer was little known and practised in recent times until the publication in the west around 1925 of *The Way of a Pilgrim*. The nineteenth century Russian pilgrim who wrote this book speaks of his discovery of the secret of uninterrupted prayer. De Mello is credited with introducing Indian Christians to the use of the Jesus Prayer.[47]

The Jesus Prayer consists of the words: 'Lord Jesus Christ, Son of God, have mercy on me, a sinner'. While mentally repeating these words, one is invited to bring one's attention into the area in the chest towards which one instinctively points when one says 'me'. This focusing of attention on the heart and centre of one's being explains the term 'prayer of the heart' by which this way of praying is also known. In time one's practice of the prayer is accompanied by a special sensation at the heart centre. Paying attention to the varying moods of that sensation helps one avoid an over-cerebral approach to meditation and also facilitates perseverance in the Jesus Prayer. In the words of one of its great teachers, Theophan the Recluse (1815–1894): 'so long as the mind remains in the head, where thoughts jostle one another, it has no time to concentrate on one thing. But when attention descends into the heart, it attracts all the powers of the soul and body into one point there'.[48]

De Mello praises the tradition of the Jesus Prayer particularly for the reason that – unlike so much of the classical literature which tells us about prayer – it teaches us how to pray.[49] He also notes that St Ignatius of Loyola taught his retreatants to recite a prayer formula to the rhythm of their breathing – and that in fact is the way De Mello himself advocates practising the Jesus Prayer.[50] It was De Mello's opinion that this type of breath mantra and the practice of praying the Name of God in a repetitive way ultimately came from Hindu India.[51] If this is correct it would point to a common root in classical yoga for the techniques associated with the Jesus Prayer as well as the *tantric approach to mantra.

JNANA YOGA

As mentioned in the previous chapter, *jnana yoga aims at awakening the mind of the practitioner to a mystical realisation of the oneness of all things. There is no fool-proof system whereby one can grasp enlightenment of this kind. Spiritual masters over the centuries have used indirect methods such as a gesture, a touch, a riddle or a paradox to trigger in their disciples a deeper awareness of spiritual reality. Story is one such means of helping spiritual aspirants to open up and become receptive to mystical insight. Jesus in the Gospels comes across as a masterly storyteller who used particular forms, especially parables and allegories, to awaken his listeners to the deepest truths.

In his seminars and workshops De Mello was known as a speaker who was not afraid to jolt the consciousness of his listeners and at times even to shock them. His reasons for doing this were to challenge and break down accepted patterns of thought and to induce self-questioning. In the words of one observer 'he challenged everyone to question, to explore, to get out of prefabricated patterns of thought and behaviour, away from stereotypes, and to dare to be one's true self ...'[52]

Story, paradox and the challenging question have for centuries been part of the tradition of *jnana yoga or 'yoga of knowledge'. What is attempted is the breaking down of superficial, self-complacent mental attitudes in order to become more open to the true knowledge (jnana) that lies within one and which is beyond all words, images and concepts (namarupa). Thus is one brought to an awareness of one's true self – understood within the Vedantic tradition to be *atman/*brahman and ultimate Reality.

ABHISHIKTANANDA AND JNANA YOGA

Henri Le Saux (1910–1973) was a French Benedictine monk who came to the Diocese of Tiruchirapalli in South India in 1948. In collaboration with Fr Jules Monchanin (1895–1957), he aimed to work towards developing a form of Christian monasticism that would be attuned to the culture of India. In 1949 the two men visited Mount Arunachala, just outside the town of Tiruvannamalai, where Le Saux had what he described as a spiritual awakening. This came about as a result of meeting the great Hindu master, Sri Ramana Maharshi (1879–1950), known as 'the sage of Tiruvannamalai'. In 1950 Monchanin and Le Saux established Saccidananda ashram at Shantivanam or 'the Forest of Peace' on the banks of the Kavery, one of India's holy rivers. With the launching of the ashram, they both adopted Indian names – Le Saux's being *Abhishiktananda* or 'bliss of the anointed one'.

Many Hindu ascetics lived in caves round the base of Arunachala. Seeing in them a parallel to the early Christian hermits who lived in the deserts of the eastern Mediterranean, Abhishiktananda became convinced that the future of Christian monastic life in India would have to come through profound dialogue with Hindu *sannyasis* such as these. During the years 1950 to 1957 he divided his time between Shantivanam and Arunachala. He began to adopt a rigorously simple lifestyle and at Arunachala spent prolonged periods of retreat in a cave. In 1955 he became a disciple of another Hindu teacher, Swami Gnanananda and through him formally undertook the life of *sannyasa* or spiritual renunciation in the Indian tradition.

From 1958 onwards Abhishiktananda began to travel extensively in the north of India, particularly in and around Banares, Hardwar and Rishikesh – age-old centres for pilgrimage, worship and monasticism located on the banks of the Ganges, India's most sacred river. In 1960 he had a very simple hermitage built at Uttarkashi in the mountainous terrain further up the Ganges. From then on he spent as much time there as he could, living in solitude, his nearest neighbours being other *sannyasis*. In 1968 he handed over the running of Saccidananda ashram to

Fr Bede Griffiths, an English Benedictine who, like himself, had been drawn into dialogue with Indian holy men. From then until his death in 1973, Abhishiktananda based himself in Uttarkashi. These last five years of his life were particularly productive in terms of writing and in inspiring the growing movement of inculturation which was being undertaken in the Indian Church following the Second Vatican Council.

Shortly before he died, Abhishiktananda was involved in the initiation of a young Frenchman, Marc Chaduc into the state of *sannyasa. This ecumenical Hindu/Christian ceremony was administered jointly by Abhishiktananda and Swami Chidananda, head of the Sivananda ashram in Rishikesh. The newly initiated Swami Ajatananda – as Marc was to be called – was meant to be a living symbol of the form monasticism was to take in India. In Abhishiktananda's words: 'the Hindu swami coopted him into the host of monks and seers of India, and I united him with the succession of monks that goes back to the Desert Fathers, and behind that to Elijah, the great monk-prophet of the Old Testament'.[1]

Following Abhishiktananda's death in 1973, Chaduc and another cherished disciple, Carmelite Sister Therese Lemoine, were left to carry on his vision. The outcome in each case was to prove tragic. In September 1976 Lemoine vanished from her hermitage at Brahmapuri on the banks of the Ganges. The door was found open, suggesting she had intended to return. Then in April 1977 Chaduc disappeared from the simple hut he had been living in at Kaudiyala near the Ganges above Rishikesh. No trace of either has been found since that time.[2]

SPIRITUALITY AND ADVAITA

Of all the Christians who have entered into dialogue with Hinduism in this century, Abhishiktananda is remarkable not only for the depth of his knowledge of the Indian Scriptures, but also for the degree to which he lived the Hindu ideal of *sannyasa. From his later writings it is clear that he had an energetic inner life, inspired by the *upanishads no less than the Gospels. His inculturation came about only gradually over the years that he spent in India. This point is illustrated by a small incident that he described in a letter. About a year after his arrival, he was embarrassed during a visit to a Hindu temple when his Christian con-science prevented him from accepting blessed flowers and fruit from the hands of the Brahmin priest.[3]

Central to the matured spirituality of Abhishiktananda's later years was what he described as his experience of *advaita* or 'non-duality'. Within Hinduism *advaita* is thought of as a kind of intuitive knowing or awareness that is beyond all rational thought. It is the state of Self-re-alisation spoken of in the *upanishads*, in passages such as: 'thou art that' in the *Chandogya* *upanishad* (6.8.7) where 'thou' refers to each human person and 'that' to the universal Self (*atman*).[4]

The Vedantic tradition holds that the experience of *advaita* goes far beyond anything to be found in any conventional religion. However – and Abhishiktananda recognised this – *vedanta* does not discount entire-ly the use of sacred images, rituals and spiritual ideas. These are accept-ed as highly effective in making people aware of and open to the reality of God. Nevertheless, they can only take us so far. In themselves they remain at the level of signs and to confuse them with ultimate reality would be to fall into a form of idolatry.[5] Only through *advaita* can there truly be knowledge of the 'Real' or of God.

Abhishiktananda believed that the experience of non-duality is not confined to those who are able and willing to study the *upanishads* and make them their own. Rather 'the discovery of the deepest centre of be-ing and of the self is a possibility for every human consciousness ...'[6] Nor does the nature of the experience depend on a person's religious tradition. *Advaita* is one and the same reality whether a person be Hindu, Buddhist or Christian. In fact, he says, the *upanishadic* experience has nothing to do with any religion whatever, being as it is the ultimate awakening of the human spirit.[7] Its foundation is more universal than that of the Biblical experience, which is based on a historical person, Jesus. What spiritual seekers are called into is that level of knowledge and being wherein one knows oneself as 'not other than' God. And on this basis Abhishiktananda makes a startling interpretation of the per-sonal relationship between Jesus and the Father as presented in the Gospels. He asserts that what Jesus experienced in his life of prayer was nothing other than *advaita* at a most profound level. In attempting to put words on his experience of 'not two', the best image Jesus could find was that of the intimacy of a father with his beloved son: 'Jesus experienced such a closeness to God – probably the very same as is revealed in the advaitic experience – that he exploded the biblical idea of "Father and Son of God" to the extent of calling God "Abba", i.e., the name which in Aramaic only the one who is "born from" him can say to anyone. But the term "Son" is only imagery, and I fear the theologians have treated this image too much as an absolute ...'[8]

JNANA YOGA AND CHRISTIANITY

Abhishiktananda understands the term 'yoga' to mean 'methods, either physiological or psychological, which can help man to enter upon and travel safely on the way of silence ... As traditionally understood, yoga is a discipline whose essential aim is to bring the mind to complete quiet and silence'.[9] It aims at nothing short of emptying the mind. In this regard he echoes the definition given in the classical yoga of Patanjali: 'the restraint of the processes of the mind'.

However, for Abhishiktananda this is not simply a question of practising silence or mind-emptying for its own sake. Based on what he learnt from Sri Ramana Maharshi and on his own experience he understands the practice of this yogic silence primarily as a means for preparing a person for the experience of *advaita. This can take place only 'in the intimacy of the guru-disciple relationship'.[10] He does not intend to suggest that *advaita is there for the taking by human effort whether of disciple or master. In keeping with this he has little time for prayer techniques or even the discipline of set times for meditation. In reality the *advaitic experience is altogether beyond physical or psychological technique and comes about only as an act of grace or as gift.[11]

Traditionally the form of yoga that is used as preparation for *advaita has been described as *jnana yoga or the 'yoga of knowledge'. This involves quietening the mind through the practice of deep inner silence. Ramana Maharshi advocated a technique which he called 'Self-enquiry'. This involves relentlessly putting to oneself the question: 'who am I?' in order to 'reveal the truth that neither the ego nor the mind really exists'.[12] This leads to a realisation of one's true identity unclouded by 'mind' or 'ego', namely: 'pure undifferentiated Being or the Self or the Absolute'.[13]

The attainment of *advaita* is the quest of all Vedantists, going back at least to Shankara (788–820), the great philosopher-saint of that school. What can be said about this ego-less 'I' or *atman/*brahman* is not expressible in the language of philosophy or theology. Probably the closest one can get in terms of language is through metaphor, particularly as found in the poetry of Shankara himself:

> I am not born; how can there be either birth or death for me?
> I am not the vital air; how can there be either hunger of thirst for me?
> I am not the mind, the organ of thought and feeling; how can there be
> either sorrow or delusion for me?
> I am not the doer; how can there be either bondage or release for me?
> I am the Peaceful One, whose form is self-effulgent, powerful radiance.
> I am neither a child, a young man, nor an ancient; nor am I of any caste ...[14]

Lines like the above do more than simply express something of the reality of the experience of *advaita*. According to some Vedantists, they can be used as instruments to bring about that very state. In the words of Heinrich Zimmer:

> The grandiose monotony of these stanzas (to be repeated silently, relentlessly, in the solitary hours of meditation, as aids to the serious intent to break past the barriers of judgement; not to be read sensitively, from some anthology) ... The stanzas are to be memorised and meditated upon; one is to be imbued with the attitude they instil. Their mind-destroying paradox, boldly stated, endlessly repeated, is an instrument of guidance to the distant shore of transcendental peace.[15]

The experience of what happens in this practice of *jnana* yoga can be interpreted in various ways. From the Christian standpoint one might say with Abhishiktananda: 'such quiet and silence alone make it possible for the Holy Spirit to work freely in the soul'.[16] However, he goes further than this. 'Yoga in itself aims at arresting the mental process of forming ideas, and then at the total disappearance of all images whatever, including even inner verbalisation, whether they be Hindu, Buddhist or Christian'.[17] With the stopping of the mental processes 'the deep power or light which normally lies hidden and inactive within every man rises up and shines forth by itself'.[18] The aim of yoga is 'the preparation of man for the ultimate encounter with himself, as explained by Vedanta, and for the ultimate encounter with the Father in the oneness of the

Holy Spirit, as Christian mystics indubitably know'.[19]

The above may seem very remote from most people's everyday lives and to be an agenda for only a few 'professional' contemplatives. Abhishiktananda however, would see the doctrines and rituals of all the major religions – Christianity not excepted – as no longer capable of underpinning human survival and sanity in the present age. From now on the experience of the inner Self beyond all 'names and forms' (*namarupa*) is going to be a necessity for modern men and women. 'In the frightening whirl of contemporary evolution the only point on which a man can stand without being constantly in danger of losing his foothold and being washed away no one knows where, is that very central and fundamental experience'.[20]

WAS ABHISHIKTANANDA A MONIST?

Most English language commentaries on the *vedanta* use the term 'monism' as equivalent to the Sanskrit *advaita* and thus view the *upanishads* as presenting a monistic philosophy.[21] Monism, which is derived from the Greek word *monos* meaning 'one', has been defined as 'the philosophy that seeks to explain all that is in terms of a single reality'.[22] As such it conflicts with a significant tenet of Christianity, namely, the distinction between various grades of being. The question therefore has to be raised as to whether Abhishiktananda, in plunging so unreservedly into the experience of *advaita*, assented also to the monistic philosophy.

Not all scholars make a simple identification between *advaita* and monism. For one commentator *advaita* is 'a process of subtle reasoning' which 'differs from both monism and pantheism'.[23] For another 'the merely quantitative problem of the one and many of dialectical reason does not apply to the realm of ultimate reality'.[24] Abhishiktananda would certainly use the term *advaita* in this more profound sense. Moreover, he goes on further to explain how over the centuries the texts of the *upanishads* came to be interpreted in a monistic sense. The great philosopher Shankara was unwittingly to provide a catalyst for this process.

Shankara is universally recognised as the most authoritative commentator within the Vedantic tradition. Abhishiktananda compares his role within *vedanta* to that of Thomas Aquinas within the Christian tradition. While they each 'bring out the true sense of their respective Scriptures', nevertheless 'each of them strives to find in them the general lines of his theological system rather than to discover the "Sitz im Leben" (original situation) of a given text'.[25] Shankara and his school used the concepts of monistic philosophy to argue against rival schools of philosophy such as those of the Buddhists. This did not in any way interfere with his fundamental understanding of the *upanishadic* texts which sprung more from his mystical experience than from his philosophical genius. For Shankara the *upanishads* remained something much richer and broader than merely a source for a philosophical standpoint. However, in subsequent centuries there were commentators and writers who without sharing in his profound spirituality, repeated his philosophical formulae. It was this, according to Abhishiktananda, that led to what he terms 'the ossification of the Upanishadic tradition'.[26]

Abhishiktananda believes that the reader who turns to the texts of the *upanishads* themselves will find a richness and variety not comprehensible in philosophical terms. He will be drawn – as Abhishiktananda himself was drawn – 'to follow for himself the meandering course of the rishi's thought'.[27] By so doing in an appropriate context of faith and under the direction of his guru, he will be better disposed to receive the graced breakthrough that Abhishiktananda understands by the term *advaita*.

Abhishiktananda's primary concern is not to present a theology or philosophy. He writes rather out of his own mystical experience. For him and for others like him the sense of personal identity with the universal Self spoken about in the *upanishads* is regarded as altogether beyond the realm of rational thought. He declares that the experience of *advaita* takes the mystical person to a state that is deeper than anything that can be known intellectually even in the most sacred religious scriptures, beyond *namarupa* or 'names and forms'.[28] And for this experience there are no philosophical pre-requisites, monist or otherwise.

WAS ABHISHIKTANANDA A GNOSTIC?

In his own person, and in the way his life developed during his twenty-four years in India, Abhishiktananda embodied a profound encounter between Christianity and Hinduism. His vision, particularly towards the end of his life, was of a synthesis higher than the usual conceptions of either of these world religions – a synthesis which would in fact take up all that was best in every religion.

He envisaged a hierarchy of spiritual development. First, there is the 'religious way' in which he specifically includes 'the spiritual heights of Christianity with its faith in the resurrection and eternal life.' The second stage is the philosophical one, exemplified in the Stoics. The philosopher will consider the consolations of religion as mere myths. What matters is thought and will. Finally, after the saint and the philosopher comes the sage, who 'has realised, and not only imagined or thought, that there is a level of being, of truth, of Self', in which he is beyond and untouched by all dualities or pairs of opposites such as security/insecurity, death/no death etc.. Abhishiktananda holds that this intuition is upheld by three traditions: the *upanishads, Buddhism and Taoism.[29]

Abhishiktananda's notion of stages in the development of the human spirit culminating in the experience of *advaita is not new. Rather, it echoes an ancient pattern of thinking within the Vedantic tradition. This thinking viewed other Indian religious schools such as *bhakti yoga and Buddhism as unenlightened – valuable only as earlier phases of a spiritual progression which would find its fulfilment only in the *vedanta. It is evident that over the centuries the Vedantists have had an unflattering opinion of these less developed forms of religion. They saw other, earlier parts of the *vedas as being suitable for 'inferior types of aspirants, whereas the teachings of the upanishads were intended only for superior aspirants who had transcended the limits of sacrificial duties and actions ...'[30] Vedantists represent a dominant intellectual elite within contemporary Hinduism. To this day they tend to regard belief in, and practice of loving devotion to, a personal God as approximating to the lower levels of knowledge described by Shankara. The serious disciple is called to transcend this 'convenient truth of a personal monotheism'.[31]

According to Abhishiktananda the meeting between Christianity and the religions of the east will take place, not by means of theological debate, but through a shared contemplative experience. He saw this dialogue as a most pressing need for the Church in the present age. Eastern religious experience, particularly as represented in the *vedanta*, challenges the value of the Church's theology and ministry – what he terms 'its mental and social expressions, the whole sphere of the *namarupa*'. The basis of the challenge is Hinduism's deep spiritual experience – and the stakes are high. According to Abhishiktananda, if Christianity fails to meet this challenge, it runs the risk of losing its claim to universality and of being 'reduced to a particular religious sect which would be remembered in history as having usefully catered for twenty centuries to the religious needs of one area of the civilised world'.[32]

The challenge which Vedantic Hinduism poses to the Christian Church parallels one that the Church has had to face in the past. In the early years of the Church's history, *gnosis* was the term used for an esoteric revelation 'available only to the elect few who are awakened to the inner divine nature that separates them from the material and perceptible cosmos...' *Gnosis* is the Greek word for 'knowledge'and is broadly equivalent to the Sanskrit *jnana*. Gnosticism, the philosophy based on gnosis, 'claims a truth that is not found by human reason or in the exoteric religious traditions of humanity'.[33] For both gnosticism and *vedanta*, there are two kinds of people: those who have been awakened to 'knowledge' and so are 'saved' or 'realised' – and those do not yet possess 'knowledge' and must rely instead on exoteric or formal religion. Gnosticism was condemned as heresy by a Church which – following the commandment of Jesus – put the primary emphasis on love rather than knowledge.

THE UNCONCERNED SELF

The Self (*atman/*brahman*) with which the Vedantist 'knows' himself to be identified, remains serenely uninvolved and unconcerned with the world and the drama of individual people's lives. The Vedic philosophy represents the Self as being in control of the phenomenal world 'and yet, simultaneously, as the unconcerned witness of it all'.[34] Whereas Christians believe in an incarnate God, i.e., a God who takes on human flesh as a real human being, Vedantists believe that salvation comes only through a person disincarnating from the entire material world – a process which takes many life-times to complete. Against this background a number of serious questions have to be put to the programme of dialogue – even fusion – espoused by Abhishiktananda. Is there a danger that it might undermine the traditional concern and involvement of Christian believers in people's entire well-being – material as well as spiritual? Again in the context of a spirituality where the entire focus is on one single existing Being, is there room for such a thing as love between God and human beings or among human beings themselves? Finally, what effect did the living of this spirituality over some twenty years have on Abhishiktananda himself?

Despite his exemplary life, a number of Christian observers of how Abhishiktananda's attitudes developed in the later years of his life, have expressed some unease about his intense preoccupation with the *advaitic* experience. Their concern was that this experience may have been drawing him away from the Gospel experience.

He seemed to be losing the sense of concrete human suffering and joy as the place where Christ's death and resurrection are experienced. One of his correspondents over many years was Anne-Marie Stokes, a fellow-worker with Dorothy Day in the Catholic Worker movement in the United States. She came to visit Abhishiktananda in the final year of his life. Her comments on the meeting reveal something about his frame of mind at that time: 'We differed a good deal about suffering and its impact, and suddenly he said an extraordinary thing: "I do not know either evil or suffering". We discussed our friend, the worker-priest, of whom he had become more critical: "he is too much in love with Christ, he will have to lose him to find him". At which I would retort that, incarnated among brutal and rather materialistic men, this priest had to look for Christ's face, hidden in the crowd. He would not believe in the contemplative potentiality of sorrow ...'[35]

BEDE GRIFFITHS AND
SHANTIVANAM

Bede Griffiths was born in 1906 in southern England into an upper-middle class Anglican family. However, as a boy he found the sense of God's presence more in the beauty of nature than in Church. On finishing his schooling he went to Magdalen College, Oxford. There friendship with his tutor, the writer C. S. Lewis, sparked his interest in Christianity. At the same time he began to read some of the classical religious literature of the east, including the *Bhagavad Gita* and the *Tao Te Ching*. This was to be the beginning of a life-long study.

On graduating in 1929, together with two of his college friends he began to live a life of radical simplicity in a cottage in the Cotswolds. They were inspired by an ideal that was romantic and intellectual. For Bede the experiment precipitated a spiritual crisis which was resolved in an encounter with God and his joining the Catholic Church in 1931. Soon after, in 1933, he joined the Benedictine community at Prinknash Abbey in South Wales.[1] For the next 20 years he served in several capacities in Prinknash and also in Farnborough Abbey. In 1955 he travelled to India with the aim of helping to establish a Benedictine community there.

For two years Bede lived at a monastery near Bangalore and it was there that he began his process of serious dialogue with Hinduism. This led to his joining Fr Francis Mahieu, a Belgian Cistercian, in founding Kurisumala ashram in Kerala. He remained there for about ten years and in 1968 took over the running of Saccidananda ashram from Abhishiktananda, who was leaving permanently for his hermitage in the Himalayas.

For the remainder of his life Bede was based at Shantivanam. Under his guidance the ashram thrived as a place of welcome and dialogue for people of all nationalities and beliefs. He travelled extensively, lecturing in Europe, America and Australia as well as in India. He wrote some ten books plus hundreds of articles. The principal goal of his work was to deepen the level of understanding between Christians and members of other world religions, especially Hinduism and Buddhism.

Bede Griffiths suffered a major stroke in 1990. However, he recovered sufficiently to resume work, including a final international lecture tour in 1991. He died on 13 May 1993.

THE FOREST OF PEACE

Shantivanam, the name by which Saccidananda ashram is most widely known, means literally 'forest of peace'. Many of those who have stayed at the ashram have testified to the extraordinarily peaceful atmosphere of the place. This is in part due to its beautiful natural setting beside the river Kavery, its buildings of brown brick half-concealed among groves of coconut palms and banana trees. Although Shantivanam is just a five minute walk from a main road, within a few moments of arriving there, one has a sense of being enveloped in an oasis of stillness.

Life in the ashram is simple. The western pilgrim in particular will have little difficulty appreciating that the word ashram has a secondary meaning as 'a place of mortification'.[2] Its vegetarian food is very basic, although adequate quantities of rice, chapattis and milk are served, the latter from the ashram's own cows. Accommodation is in austere one and two bed cells, some of which are in the form of small, single-roomed thatched huts. It was in one of these, at the forest's edge, that Fr Bede lived. The refectory is totally without furniture, except for light reed matting on which one sits in silence while eating. A compact but substantial library of books and magazines on eastern and western theology and spirituality testifies to the intellectual stature of Fr Bede and his predecessors at Shantivanam.

The ashram's chapel is intended to remind one of a Hindu temple. Its cave-like sanctuary opens out into a forest of stone pillars that seem to merge into the nearby trees. At the times of prayer saffron-clad monks and other worshippers sit cross-legged on the floor. Here the daily Indian-rite Eucharist is celebrated with Sanskrit chants to the accompaniment of Indian musical instruments such as sitar and tabla. Extracts from the *vedas, *upanishads, Sufi and Buddhist mystics, as well as Biblical readings, are incorporated into the Morning and Evening liturgies. All the services are rich in symbolism whose origins are Hindu rather than Christian: *arati* (the slow circular movement of lighted camphor) before the Blessed Sacrament, chanting of the sacred syllable *Om* and the placing of *tilak*, coloured powder or paste on the worshippers' foreheads as a sign of welcome. There are two one-hour meditation periods daily, coinciding with dawn and sunset.

The most striking feature of Shantivanam, however, was the personality of its guru. Bede followed in the footsteps of Fathers Monchanin and Le Saux in seeking to make the ashram a meeting point between the religions of the east and of the west. In this respect he was outstandingly successful and attracted a wide spectrum of visitors. Indian clergy and religious came in search of spiritual deepening and guidance in the area of religious inculturation for themselves and the communities they served. Foreign visitors ranged from traditional Catholics to people of no religious affiliation. Some were 'into' yoga, zen, t'ai ch'i or other forms of eastern or New Age exercise. Many were aliens from what they perceived to be a moribund Church in their home country. All were searching for some deeper meaning to their lives and cheerfully accepted the privations of ashram life in pursuit of that aim. They responded to the gentle wisdom and evident sanctity of the elderly guru. A few requested and received Baptism from him. Many were reconciled to the Church. All came to at least view the Church in a less negative way. As one convent-educated young woman, a former Catholic, put it: 'At least I can respect Christianity now'.

Shantivanam under the direction of Bede Griffiths, was no mere refuge from life's responsibilities, but rather a focus and catalyst for the spiritual and material renewal of society. He placed great emphasis on the revitalisation of village life, particularly in the district around the ashram. Thus the ashram community has initiated or inspired several works of social improvement. It was customary for the people of the countryside to show their appreciation of these activities by feting Fr Bede on the occasion of his birthday during the latter years of his life. The celebrations in his honour took the form of open-air functions with music and dance followed by dinner. To the local people, both Christian and Hindu, Fr Bede was a *mahatma*, or 'great soul'.

In his writings and in the daily talks that he gave in the ashram temple Bede Griffiths tended to look for common ground between theological positions that at first sight appeared irreconcilable. Typical of his approach would be to say: 'At the superficial level these two points of view are contradictory. So, we have to go to a deeper level to try to find a common standpoint'. Two examples of how he dealt with doctrinal conflicts between the world religions are as follows:

1) The term after which Shantivanam ashram is named is composed of three words: *sat* (being), *cit* (knowledge or consciousness) and *ananda* (bliss or joy). *Saccidananda like *brahman refers to the one, eternal, never-changing reality, what in the west one would term 'Supreme Being' or 'God'. However, *saccidananda goes further than *brahman in that it recognises three fundamental aspects in the Divine – Being, Knowledge and Bliss. This triad invites comparison with the Christian Trinity of Father, Son and Holy Spirit.[3]

The Christian doctrine of the Trinity is based on the New Testament. According to Bede, it was developed in terms of philosophical categories such as 'person', 'nature' and 'essence' which were part of the Greek culture with which the early Church had to come to terms. Centuries later St Thomas Aquinas summarised this tradition in his full-blown trinitarian theology. However, there is no fundamental reason why the Christian doctrine of the Trinity – and indeed the whole corpus of Christian revelation – cannot equally well be viewed and expressed in the categories of eastern thought and experience. This task, Bede believed, is one of the great challenges facing Christianity today. His work, like the work of some others studied in this book, was an attempt to respond to that challenge. For Bede, the Christian experience of God might then be summarised as *saccidananda – Being, Knowledge and Bliss, terms that would not be out of step with orthodox theology. As Bede expresses it, 'We could then speak of the Son as the *Cit*, the knowledge of the Father, the self-consciousness of eternal Being ... we could speak of the Spirit as the *Ananda*, the Bliss or Joy of the Godhead ... the Love which unites Father and Son in the non-dual Being of the Spirit'.[4]

2) A more revealing example of Bede's efforts to find common

ground between the theologies of east and west is to be found in his treatment of the Hindu notion of *advaita* or 'non-dualism'. This topic was looked at in some detail in the previous chapter in the contexts of Abhishiktananda's spirituality. It was seen then that *advaita* does not equate simply with monism and specifically pantheistic monism – a point that Bede also stresses.[5] Pantheistic monism is the philosophical theory that everything that exists must be understood in terms of one single reality that is not other than God. Bede's handling of the question is distinct from Abhishiktananda's and tells us quite a bit about his approach to conflict resolution.

If *advaita* were to be equated with pantheistic monism, then it would indeed be opposed to the Christian teaching that everything created is distinct from God and that there are distinct forms and grades of being. Bede explains that a correct understanding of the *advaita* doctrine holds that whatever truly exists in this world, exists eternally in *brahman*. Outside and independent of *brahman* it does not exist in reality and is mere *maya* or 'illusion'. Our human knowledge, conditioned as it is by the senses, makes things appear to exist distinctly and independently, separated in time and space. In God, on the other hand, there is no such thing as separation or division – this according to both Shankara, who was the leading exponent of the *advaita* system, and Thomas Aquinas. Aquinas taught moreover that 'Everything – and every person – exists eternally in God as God'.[6] To conclude his argument, Bede asserts that *advaita* is 'a truth as Catholic as it is Hindu'.[7]

INCARNATION – ONE OR MANY?
The question of *samsara*, or rebirth is one of the most intractable questions dividing Hinduism and Buddhism on the one hand, and Christianity, Islam and Judaism on the other. How can one reconcile the doctrine of successive reincarnations or transmigrations with the teaching that one is given just one opportunity to live and die on this planet? Bede's response was to remind us that we do not exist and live and die as detached individuals but are ultimately part of one organic whole that develops and grows throughout history. This contention of Bede's that the different parts of the universe are fundamentally interdepen-

dent is well supported by significant figures in twentieth century science and philosophy.[8] Bede, however, relies particularly on two contemporary physicists, who have become significant voices within the New Age movement – Fritjof Capra and David Bohm. Capra points out that quantum physics can operate only on the assumption that no part of the universe functions independently of the others.[9] Bohm uses the complex imagery of a hologram to describe the universe. Bede presents Bohm's theory more simply by saying that the universe is 'an integrated whole, which is "folded up", as it were, and what we see is the explication, the "unfolding" of this whole'.[10]

The holistic picture of the universe as described above stands in contrast to the mechanistic model of the universe which has held sway within western culture from the time of Descartes until the twentieth century. This model sees matter and spirit as two quite separate and independent principles. The system of physics built up by Newton views the universe as a vast machine built up from separately existing parts. The Newtonian model of the world has driven the modern physical sciences, as well as technical and industrial progress and *laissez faire* enterprise. Carried to the extremes as it was in the nineteenth and twentieth century, it left little room in western culture for spirituality, poetry or communing with nature. According to Bede, the progressive working out of this way of thinking now poses very serious threats to humanity and the environment. It will have to be better balanced with a more holistic picture of reality. Holism stresses community rather than individualism in human affairs and views the natural world as one ordered entity rather than as a collection of many independent parts. The holistic view of the world is widespread in eastern societies and in less developed parts of the world. It is also the view that prevailed in Europe before the Renaissance. It is well represented within the Christian tradition by, for example, the world-view of Aquinas. Aquinas attributes the notion of wholeness properly speaking only to the whole universe and not to any individual part of Creation.[11]

Speaking from the holistic standpoint, Bede asserts that it is not the isolated unit of humanity that dies and is reborn, but rather the whole of humanity. He goes on to quote the statement of Shankara: 'The Lord is the only Transmigrator'.[12] The divine Self incarnates into each human being. As people are born and die the Self continually reincarnates, passing from life to life. Because of the Incarnation of Jesus, Christ is this Self who incarnates, not just in each human person, but in the entire Creation. The true meaning of the Christian Incarnation is found in the progressive taking up of the whole of humanity and the whole universe into the life of God.[13] However, Bede does not gloss over a fundamental difficulty in the Hindu doctrine of *samsara, namely the attitude of fatalism that seems to accompany belief in it. This, he believes, lies behind the lackadaisical approach to people's material needs that seems to characterise Indian society. As he puts it: 'I cannot help feeling that the present situation in India, with its masses of poor, illiterate people suffering from disease and being left to die in the streets, really stems from this basic philosophy – all are caught in this wheel of *samsara'.[14]

JNANA YOGA AND ADVAITIC EXPERIENCE

Bede's method of dialogue may strike some Christian readers in particular as little more than intellectual sleight of hand designed to make real contradictions between world religions disappear. One commentator has used the expression 'flirting with paradox' in connection with his approach.[15] However, there is more to Bede's methodology than simply working at the level of ideas, and that is the way he introduces into his theology the dimension of mystical experience. What is involved here is a highly innovative form of what Indian thinkers would term *jnana yoga or 'yoga of knowledge'. Bede's approach to the different understandings of mythology as between the Hindu and the Judaeo-Christian traditions will now be looked at. It will be seen that the key to this difference lies in the two traditions' different philosophies of time.

The stories associated with Jesus, such as his virgin birth, his death and resurrection, his ascension into heaven and his ultimate return in glory, all have a historical character. Each is believed to take place in a particular place and at a particular moment in time. Place and time and each individual person are highly significant in the context of the Christian vision of the world. God's purpose for each and all is being progressively realised over the passage of time and world history.

Whereas Christian mythology implies a linear view of time, the

Hindu myth, on the other hand, is based on a cyclical view of time. Unlike Jesus, who is a very definite historical figure, the *avataras or incarnations of Hindu deities such as Rama and Krishna, are legendary or semi-historical figures. They all reflect one and the same unchanging, timeless, eternal Reality: *saccidananda. Even in the case of the historically most known of the Indian *avataras – Gautama the Buddha – his historicity is not deemed to be of any great importance. Time may indeed march on. Different *avataras come into the world to offer spiritual solace to humankind in different epochs. Yet in all of this the world is going nowhere or at most going round in circles. Historical individuals, nations, events as such are not significant. They are all part of *maya, an appearance of reality that has no ultimate significance.[16]

Bede asks rhetorically: how can these two revelations be reconciled: on the one hand, 'the cosmic revelation of the infinite, timeless Being manifesting in this world of time and change, but ultimately unaffected by it' and, on the other hand, 'the Christian revelation of God's action in history, of the one, eternal Being acting in time and history and bringing this world of time and change into union with himself'? In response he offers no philosophical solution, nothing based on reason or science. Nevertheless, he tells us, one can begin by trying with one's mind to see as far as possible the values in each of these revelations. That is a first step. However, full harmonisation can only be found through 'going beyond the differences in an experience of "non-duality", of transcendence of all dualities'.[17]

This experience of non-duality or *advaita brings us to the heart of Bede's theologising. As distinct from the more philosophical concept of *advaita discussed earlier in this chapter, what is referred to here is *advaita as a 'mystical experience which underlies both the Hindu and the Christian tradition'.[18] The Christian mystical experience differs from that of Hinduism in that 'the absolute reality is experienced as revealed in Christ, in the life and death of Jesus of Nazareth'.[19] A further way in which Bede's thinking on *advaita differs for instance from that of Shankara is that Bede maintains that for the Christian a real distinction of persons remains within the *advaitic experience: 'He (Jesus) experienced Himself as one with God, the Father, and yet distinct'.[20] This preservation of distinct personal identities leaves the way open for the dimension of interpersonal love, something that is lacking in the Hindu *advaita* tradition, where the emphasis instead is on consciousness.[21]

For all traditions alike the experience of *advaita* is 'beyond all limitations of time and space, beyond word and thought'.[22] It is of course indescribable, yet the writings of mystics from every tradition indicate that they have all 'been there'. Because the state of *advaita* is beyond language and concepts, there is no room for contradiction. All who enter here are at one. Irrespective of their diverse backgrounds, they have merged at the deepest level of interpersonal and interreligious dialogue.

Like Abhishiktananda, like Ramana Maharshi and so many others, Bede has used the reasoning process as the point of departure, the trigger for the experience of *advaita*. Thus it can be seen that his methodology derives from a form of *jnana* yoga. However, he reminds us that more than reasoning is involved, since this knowledge comes from above. The path to it is 'by a radical detachment from the self, that is, from all selfish attachment to the world, the flesh and the ego'.[23] However, what appears to be unique to Bede's approach is the way he feeds the experience back into his theology and uses it to draw different ideologies together, for he is convinced that the world has need of both the eastern and the western visions of reality. The result is an integrated mystical theology balancing theory and practice, study and meditation, science and spirituality, western religion and eastern religion.

CHRISTIAN YOGAS

Unlike Abhishiktananda, Bede was not opposed to the use of the term 'Christian yoga'.[24] Saccidananda ashram, with his active encouragement, facilitated the practice of many forms of yoga. Yoga postures as preparation for meditation was for some years taught by Amaladass, Bede's disciple who, had he not predeceased Bede, might well have succeeded him as head of the ashram. Bede encouraged *bhakti* and *karma* yogas in the spirit of the *Bhagavad Gita*. These are yogas respectively of devotion and detached service of a God who 'is more, not less, than personal'.[25] In his own prayer life Bede used *mantra* yoga in the form of the Jesus prayer, 'Lord Jesus Christ, Son of God, have mercy on me, a sinner', repeated over and over. This he practised, not only during his morning and evening meditations, but continually throughout the day: 'Whenever I am not otherwise occupied or thinking of something else, the prayer goes quietly on'.[26]

Bede's interest in *tantric* yoga developed in the later decades of his life. He summed up his general understanding of *tantra* in the words: 'That by which we fall is that by which we rise'. 'We have to use the body, senses, appetites, feelings, etc., as a way to return to God'.[27] Bede's thinking on *tantric* yoga relies heavily on the study done by a fellow Camaldolese monk, Thomas Matus.[28] Like Matus, Bede concentrated his attention on that aspect of *tantra* known as *kundalini* yoga.

Bede contrasts *kundalini* yoga with the yoga of Patanjali or raja yoga, which involves the disengagement or detachment of human consciousness from matter so that it can enjoy the bliss of isolation.[29] Raja yoga involves an ascent of the human spirit away from matter. *Kundalini* (and *tantric* yoga in general), on the other hand, is earthy and works within the material world and the human body. As mentioned earlier it speaks metaphorically of the union of the god *shiva* (a mythological representation of consciousness), who resides at the top of the head, with the goddess *shakti* (representing power), who is awakened at the base of the spine and is drawn up through each of seven *cakras* or centres of psychic energy. Bede sees raja and *kundalini* yoga as complementing one another. Taken together, they constitute 'a descent of the Spirit into matter and a corresponding ascent, by which matter is transformed by the indwelling power of the spirit and the body is transfigured'.[30]

Bede finds echoes of the *shiva*/*shakti* dualism in many areas of human life. He speaks about pairings such as that of man/woman and reason/intuition, each pole of which is incomplete without the other. It is interesting that the language he uses comes from the vocabulary of *tantric* and *kundalini* yoga. For instance he writes: 'Intuition begins in the darkness of the child in the womb. It grows through the *awakening* of emotional and imaginative experience, but it eventually has to be *drawn up through* the passive intellect ... into the clear light of the mind. It is then that the *marriage* of imagination and reason ... takes place (*italics mine*)'.[31] It is evident here that Bede has in mind the upward movement of the *kundalini* *shakti* (whom elsewhere he identifies with the

Holy Spirit) through the various *cakras* to meet her consort *shiva* (consciousness) at the crown of the head.[32]

It is clear from the foregoing that Bede had deeply assimilated the *tantric* programme of seeking to overcome opposite polarities. On the larger scale one of his lifelong desires was to resolve the dichotomy between western rational scientific thinking and the more intuitive, imaginative insights of the east such as are found *par excellence* within the spiritual writings of Hinduism and Buddhism. This yearning found expression in the title of one of his best known books, *The Marriage of East and West*. A further aspiration of his was for the Church 'to construct a theology, using the philosophy of the Vedanta as its basis in the same way as the Greek Fathers and Aquinas used the philosophy of Plato and Aristotle'. These grand visions remain unrealised to date, but seem likely to be on the theological agenda for the twenty-first century.

YOGA IN CHRISTIAN ASHRAMS

Variously described as 'a settlement of disciples living with or round a guru';[1] 'a group of people who have put the effort towards God-realisation before everything else';[2] 'a state or place of intense and sustained spiritual quest for the Absolute by a group of persons around and under the guidance of a *guru*';[3] and 'a place of mortification'[4] – an ashram is essentially indefinable. Though there are thousands scattered across every region of India, and increasingly overseas as well, no two ashrams are alike. However, there are certain typical features. Ashrams tend to be peaceful places, frequently located in natural settings of great beauty. The buildings are simple. The atmosphere is one of silence, the pace of living gentle, contemplative and orientated towards God-experience. Ashram food is strictly vegetarian. There are set times for communal meditation and worship. Above all, there are one or more spiritual teachers or guides who are given the title 'Swami' or 'Guru'.

Ashrams have some points in common with Christian religious communities. However, there are also significant differences. A religious community is usually founded as a result of a decision taken by a higher Church authority such as a bishop or the congregation that will run the community. An ashram, on the other hand, is 'born' only when one or more disciples come to a guru and express a desire to join with and learn from him or her. It is not affiliated or under the control of some higher religious jurisdiction.[5] Secondly, whereas religious communities admit to their ranks only those who intend making a life-long commitment to seek God according to the rule of that particular community, ashrams have a more flexible concept of 'belonging'. Fully initiated *sannyasis* (ascetics) may spend all of their lives in one ashram, or may move between ashrams, or opt to live alone as hermits. Non-initiates and visitors can arrange to stay in an ashram for long or short periods. The only requirements are that they be in some sense 'God-seekers' and that their behaviour be in keeping with ashram traditions. Thus, a complete ban on meat-eating, alcohol, drugs and smoking is the universal norm since, to the Indian mind, all of these are incompatible with any serious spiritual quest.

Prior to the twentieth century ashrams were a characteristically Indian institution. Their religious context was exclusively Hindu or Buddhist. Recent decades have witnessed three developments that are widening significantly the spectrum of people who are influenced by life in and around ashrams. The first is the attraction that Indian ashrams are increasingly holding for people from western countries. It is estimated that several hundred thousand young westerners are in India at any one time, many of them actively seeking spiritual experiences of one kind or another. Christian groups have been attempting to minister to these young people through specially set up ashrams.[6] Secondly, ashrams are being established outside India, particularly in North America and Europe. Many new religious and New Age movements in the west – including most of those described in this book – operate through ashrams and might even be described as 'ashram movements'. The other important development this century is the development of ashrams that are Christian in character. In the early 1980s one researcher, Michael O'Toole, visited no less than forty-two Christian ashrams in India and Sri Lanka and described each of them in some detail. And there were others that, because of constraints of time, money and stamina, he was unable to visit.[7] The oldest Christian ashram, Christukulam in Tamil Nadu was founded as long ago as 1921. In more recent years Christian ashrams and ashram-like communities have been established in western countries – though they rarely describe themselves as 'ashrams'. Their number is likely to increase. Westerners, both those who go to church and those who do not, are being more and more attracted to what ashrams can provide: practical guidance in meditation and spiritual growth, and the means to prepare for these – usually yogic – that these centres offer.

Saccidananda ashram – associated with Abhishiktananda and Bede Griffiths – is one of the most important Christian ashrams in India. The remainder of this chapter will take a brief look at two other outstanding Indian Christian ashrams leaders, as well as the yogic thinking and practices of each.

D. S. Amalorpavadass was born in 1932 in Kallery near Pondicherry in South India. Having completed second-level education in 1949 he joined the Minor Seminary in Cuddalore where he stayed from 1949 to 1953 whilst studying at St Joseph's College, Tiruchirapalli. He then became a student for the priesthood at St Peter's Major Seminary in Bangalore. In spite of weak health during his seminary days, he was a brilliant student and wrote several booklets in Tamil. He was ordained as a priest in 1959, following which he joined the staff of the Regional Catechetical Centre, Tindivanam. There he published a monthly review and established a documentation centre and library. He organised many seminars all over Tamil Nadu.

From 1962 to 1965 Fr Amalor did higher studies at the *Institute Catholique* in Paris. His master's and doctoral theses were both published as books entitled respectively: *l'Inde e la rencontre du Seigneur* and *Destinee de l'Eglise dans l'Inde d'aujourdhui*. On his return to India Amalor was appointed Secretary of the Indian Bishops' Commission for Liturgy and Catechetics. More significantly in 1966 he began the work that led to the establishment of the National Biblical, Catechetical and Liturgical Centre (NBCLC) in Bangalore. Under his guidance the NBCLC was to have an enormous influence on the Catholic Church in India. Its main thrust was to build up an authentic local church rooted in India's cultural and religious heritage. Amalor continued to direct the NBCLC until 1982 when he left to give his full attention to the new directions his life's work was taking in Mysore.

The University of Mysore was the first state university in India to institute a Chair and a Department in Christianity. In 1982 Amalor was appointed the first Professor of Christianity there. However, some years earlier in 1979 he had already taken the first steps towards establishing Anjali Ashram close to the entrance to the university. The university and the ashram were the two focuses of Fr Amalor's attention for the remainder of his life, a life that was prematurely cut short by a fatal road accident in May 1990.[8]

Anjali Ashram is situated about four kilometres from Mysore city, overlooked by Chamundi Hill with its 800 year old Chamundeshwari Temple. Because of its location, thousands of Hindus pass its entrance each day on their way to have *darshan* (literally 'sight') of the gilded idol of the goddess Chamundeshwari. The spacious ashram entrance with its gates permanently open stands as an invitation to passers-by to 'come in and rest awhile'– even for as little as half and hour.

Founded in 1979, the ashram passed through several stages over the following five years or so to reach its present form. It is built along an axis perpendicular to the main road. Entering on foot one passes through a series of single-storeyed buildings in a south Indian garden setting of coconut palms and banana trees. The buildings merge into a carefully planned and cultivated environment. The first to be encountered is the *viswagopuram* (cosmic cupola), a small eight-pillared pavilion symbolising 'cosmic order and harmony'. From there one moves on to the large open rectangular *satsang mantapam* (community hall), symbolising 'social order and sharing'. This is used for meetings with groups of up to 200 people.

From the *satsang mantapam* one proceeds to the *swagata nilayam* (reception area) which provides facilities for short-term visitors, and the *atma purna nivas* which houses the chapel, library, kitchen/dining area and cells for fifteen ashram-dwellers. It is encircled by a group of ten tree-shaded cottages, each providing accommodation for an additional individual resident or visitor. Continuing along the path in a straight line, one passes by other buildings whose names and designs have spiritual significance. *Sat-cit-ananda* temple or the temple of 'being-knowledge-bliss' is at the end of the path. Its title and position are intended to signify the life that is to be found in Brahma or the Holy Trinity. The pilgrim need go no further. He has reached his goal, the supreme and ultimate reality.

Each element in the lay-out of Anjali ashram has been designed and named to express a particular meaning. This was also the case with the National Biblical Catechetical and Liturgical Centre in Bangalore, the buildings of which were also designed by Fr Amalor. Commenting on the structure of the National Centre, Amalor wrote; 'The more one looks for meaning, the more he will find it and the more the campus will appear and unfold itself as meaningful'.[9] His method of using architecture to give detailed expression to a spiritual system was repeated more than a decade later at Anjali ashram. Here too one is justified in looking for meaning at different levels in the way in which the ashram is designed and laid out.

The basic message of the plan is that the individual is invited to embark on the quest for wholeness or personal integration 'facilitated by the practice of an integrated spirituality system of India, yoga ...'[10] This is expressed by walking on the ashram's straight central path, deviating neither to the right nor to the left. In this context Amalor uses the image of an arrow 'moving non-stop towards the target, Brahman'.[11] The objective of the pilgrim's quest is symbolised in the temple which lies at the path's end. This journey to God has a number of distinct stages at any one of which the seeker is free to perform a U-turn or simply drop out to the side. The different stages in the spiritual journey are expressed in the different groups of buildings.

A rough map of the as yet incomplete ashram is contained in an early edition of *Anjali Ashram*, the official guide to the ashram, written by Amalor. On the map the ashram's looped service road looks vaguely like the outline of a human body. On this map the five main features of the complex referred to above resemble a diagram of five *cakras in the human body. The *viswa gopuram* at the bottom of the page, corresponds to the base *cakra, while the *sat-cit-ananda temple at the top has a circular path round it that makes it appear like the head of the 'body', thus reminding one of the *sahasrara *cakra. Subsequent development of the ashram buildings did not follow this plan exactly, particularly in regard to the location of the temple. Nevertheless, this earlier plan gives an important clue to Amalor's vision at the time of writing.

The architecture of Anjali ashram appears to be based on *tantric and specifically *kundalini philosophy. In its layout the ashram mirrors the human body and expresses a spirituality that is lived within the body. In common with Hindu temples, the layout also forms a *yantra* – a shape which is used in *tantric yoga as an aid to meditation. A *yantra* is 'divisible only along its vertical axis (divided horizontally, the parts are asymmetrical); this vertical orientation ... makes it a pattern for the ascending movement of *kundalini-*shakti ...'[12] As mentioned earlier, *kundalini yoga conceives of a straight central channel within the human body, along which the spiritual energy called *kundalini or *shakti has to travel through various *cakras until it meets God-consciousness or *shiva at the crown of the head. This journey is not completed for all aspirants. For most, the *kundalini energy will go no further than the first or second *cakra – symbolised by those visitors who do not reach the head, or even the heart of the ashram.

As further evidence of his interest in *tantra and *kundalini, in his earlier work at the National Centre Amalor used *kundalini symbolism in his design of the centre's chapel – a symbolism whose meaning he spelt out at that time. The tabernacle which is the chapel's central focus is located in the middle of 'the cosmic tree'. This (he wrote) represents 'the communion between God and Man, heaven and earth, in and through Jesus Christ. The *ascending energies* of the earth and the *descending energies* of heaven meet in Jesus Christ, God made man' (*italics mine*).[13] These words and the artwork they describe express the Christian mystery in the language of *kundalini yoga.

A few years later Amalor refrained from stating in his pamphlet that the plan of Anjali ashram was in part at least intended to incorporate *tantric *kundalini ideas – and perhaps with good reason. In designing the National Centre, Amalor had placed on top of the centre's chapel or temple a representation of the *Kalasam* or 'Sacred Vessel', rather than the more traditional cross. The vessel or chalice is a symbol that is common both to Hinduism and Christianity. Its erection was to prove controversial. In later writings he justified its use, but in the end acknowledged that 'in spite of this clear explanation and evidence of tradition some people continue to misinterpret it and allege that the cross, a Christian sign is replaced by *Kalasam*, a Hindu symbol'.[14] Given the fact that much *tantric practice is highly controversial even within Hinduism, it is hardly surprising that, rather than spelling out its significance in detail, Amalor might have opted to allow the layout of Anjali ashram to 'unfold itself as meaningful' to the one who looks for that meaning. In this regard he would have been echoing the *tantric yoga tradition which over the centuries has tended to transmit its practices, partly at least, in secret.

Sister Vandana

Gool Mary Dhalla was born in 1924 in Bombay to a Parsee family. She converted to Catholicism at the age of 18 while a student at Sophia

College, Bombay. A few years later she became the first Indian to join the Religious of the Sacred Heart, the Congregation of Sisters who run the college. She occupied several positions of responsibility within the congregation, including that of provincial superior of the Sisters in India.

Following the Second Vatican Council Sister Dhalla was one of a group of religious, clergy and laity who led the movement to make Catholic religious life and worship more relevant to Indian conditions. She was particularly inspired and influenced by Swami Abhishiktananda when he spoke at the National Seminar held at Bangalore in 1969. Abhishiktananda encouraged 'inculturation' of the Church in India. He also urged religious to live a simpler, open ashram-style life rather than continuing in enclosed convents. As an expression of her intent, in 1971 Gool Dhalla took the Indian name *Vandana* (meaning 'praise' or 'adoration'). She was involved that year in the re-opening of Christa Prem Seva ashram, Pune. This was originally founded in 1927 as an Anglican ashram but had been closed for some years. It was now to be an ecumenical centre run jointly by Anglican Sisters of St Mary the Virgin and Catholic Sacred Heart Sisters. Under Sister Vandana's influence particularly, it adopted a simple Indian regime in regard to food, furnishings, dress and worship. Abhishiktananda with Pandit Dadasaheb, a Hindu friend and follower of Gandhi, spent a month with the Sisters in the new ashram, initiating them in the study of the *upanishads, Bhagavad-Gita* and Indianising the Liturgy. All the members agreed that 'the ashram should be a place of prayer, research and inter-religious dialogue where anyone may come and feel at home'.[15]

From 1973 Vandana and another Sister of the Sacred Heart – Isha-priya – lived six months of each year for six years in Hindu ashrams in India, but particularly in the Sivananda ashram in Rishikesh in the Himalayan foothills. There they were welcomed and encouraged by Swami Chidananda, successor to Swami Sivananda as head of the ashram. From 1978 they occupied a small *kuttir* ('hut') of their own – thus becoming the first Christians to live in Rishikesh, a holy city for Hindus. They called their hut *Jeevan Dhara Sadhana Kuttir. Jeevan Dhara* means 'living water', while *Sadhana* implied that the *kuttir* was only for their own spiritual practice, not an ashram as yet open to all. In 1984 they were led to take the next step in establishing their own Christian ashram at Jaiharikhal, further up in the Himalayas. They named it *Jeevan Dhara Ashram*. Vandana and Ishapriya were the first women to begin a Catholic ashram in India. This ashram is fully open to women and men of all faiths and cultures. It follows Indian and Hindu traditions insofar as these are compatible with the Gospels.

Since the foundation of *Jeevan Dhara* Sister Vandana has been based at Jaiharikhal but spends part of her time giving spiritual retreats in many different countries. She also spends time at other centres of eastern spirituality, particularly at Plum Village in France, where the Vietnamese Buddhist monk, Thich Nhat Hanh has been based since receiving political asylum in that country. In recent years Vandana has acknowledged her indebtedness to Buddhist teachers like Nhat Hanh and Goenka. What she finds of particular value in teachers like these is not doctrine but method. As she puts it: 'Buddhism does not speak about God: it teaches the way to God'.[16]

In her spiritual practice and teaching Sister Vandana has used a variety of yoga techniques, whose original contexts are both Hindu and Buddhist. These include postures, breathing, meditative visualisation, mindfulness, etc. She also practises and teaches the form of yoga known as *japa ('repetition'). This is the practice of devoutly repeating one or other of the names of God. One of the best-known of her many books is *Nama Japa*, a study of the different ways in which the praying of God's name is used in Hinduism and in both eastern and western Christianity. *Japa yoga has many different expressions. The recitation of the name can be audible, whispered or silent. It can be done to the rhythm of one's breathing or with *mala* beads, the Hindu equivalent of the Rosary except that the beads can be of a different number, for example, 27, 64, 100 or 108. The name of God can be sung by oneself or in a group, sitting on the ground or dancing. There is also the form of *japa known as *likhit* (meaning 'written'). This means slowly and mindfully writing the name of God over and over again on a page, sometimes forming a pattern that can become quite intricate and beautiful. Irrespective of the particular *japa form used, it is recommended that one recite the name of God with full attention and for a definite period of time.[17]

Like Abhishiktananda and Bede Griffiths before her, Vandana believes that contemplative spirituality is the key to healing the divisions that currently exist between the religions of the world. It is meditating together – rather than theologising – that will bring about real transformation in people and promote genuine ecumenism on a global scale. Where religion is concerned her vision of the future is quite radical. She looks forward to the time when 'there will be no more Christian or Hindu or Buddhist ashrams, or any need to speak or think in terms of Hindu, Christian or Buddhist meditation, as we do today'.[18] In the next century she envisages that there could be a new type of spiritual life lived in authentic ashrams, where men and women of different faiths would live together in harmony, each religion contributing something unique to the others. She is encouraged in this hope by the fact that such communities are already beginning to flourish in western countries that might fairly be described today as 'post-Christian'. In these Hindu ashrams and Buddhist *maths* or 'monasteries' hundreds of people live in serious spiritual practice, while many more drop in for shorter periods of spiritual renewal and teaching.[19]

CONCLUSION

To ask 'can yoga be a path to God?' is a bit like asking 'how long is a piece of string?' In each case the question is not open to a simple answer, but is designed rather to provoke a search. Reflecting on the question 'how long is a piece of string?' starts one thinking about string. One visualises it in different positions. Mentally one straightens it out and places it alongside a ruler. This may have the effect of making one aware of the string's thickness, its strength, its colour and texture, the material out of which it is made and so on. In the end what one gets is not abstract information, but a 'feeling knowledge' about string and its possible uses. In a similar way these pages have been an exploration of possible and actual uses of yogic techniques in relation to spirituality and the search for God. There are a wide variety of contexts pertaining to many different religious and spiritual traditions, many centuries and many parts of the world. What has been written here hopefully catches the various 'flavours' as well as the wide variety of methods.

Whether yoga can lead a person to God or not depends on the yogic methods used but also on the particular ways they are practised by each individual. It will be evident from Part Two of this book that some yogic techniques can be physically, psychologically and spiritually hazardous. Those who intend to make use of them would be well advised to seek competent guidance. That cautionary note having been sounded, it needs to be acknowledged that in India at least, authentic religious pilgrims have for thousands of years practised one form of yoga or another. Within that spiritually rich culture, the quest for God without the practice of yoga would be inconceivable.

For those whose religious search is in the context of Christianity the relevant question is: can yoga be Christian, or can there be such a thing as 'Christian yoga'? At the present time the Christian Church in the western world is in crisis. This is partly because it is actively contradicted by rival philosophies. Of more practical significance is the fact that the Church's message is being ignored or dismissed as irrelevant by the great majority of people in countries traditionally regarded as Christian. Meanwhile New Religions and the New Age Movement are making major inroads in these same societies. The philosophies of these movements are certainly no richer than the Christian spiritual tradition. However, the situation on the ground is not being determined by the depth of wisdom or the soundness of a group's philosophy or theology. The new movements are succeeding because they engage their followers successfully at the level of experience. The question as to whether yoga can be Christian boils down to the issue of whether some yogic techniques can be adapted for use in Christian prayer and spirituality, whether they can be used to help extend a believer's head knowledge of the Faith into heart and body experience. What is being asked here is whether yogic exercises can in some way help prepare the body, the mind and the human spirit to be more receptive to the gifts of the Holy Spirit.

It is my belief that spiritual life can only be the result of divine grace and can never be acquired by any technique, yogic or other. Nevertheless, I would also maintain that some (but by no means all) yogic techniques can be beneficially utilised to dispose a person to a fuller experience of Christian prayer and living. The lives and works of Déchanet, Abhishiktananda, Bede Griffiths, De Mello, Main, Amalor, Vandana and others exemplify ways of incorporating yogic practice into Christian spirituality. This is not to say that the work of these remarkable individuals does not call for further refinement and development. But the work has been started – and with great vision and commitment. There still remains so much more in the yogic tradition to challenge men and women of faith to investigate, enter into dialogue with, experiment with and reflect on. With proper discernment, there is also much more that can safely and beneficially be practiced. The Christian Church can ill afford to ignore this challenge and opportunity as it enters its third millenium.

GLOSSARY OF KEY SANSKRIT TERMS

(MARKED WITH AN ASTERISK (*) IN THE TEXT)

Advaita: 'non-dualism', a mystical realisation of the oneness of all that exists. Opposed by *dvaita* or 'dualist' philosophy which holds for the real distinction between beings.

Aghori: yogi of the unorthodox *aghora* order whose practices, such as eating the flesh of corpses and using a skull as a drinking vessel, are intended to outrage every social convention.

Ashtanga: 'eight limbed' yoga according to Patanjali. The limbs are: restraint (*yama*), discipline (*niyama*), posture (*asana*), breath control (*pranayama*), sense withdrawal (*pratyahara*) concentration (*dharana*), meditation (*dhyana*) and ecstasy (*samadhi*).

Atman: literally 'breath', 'soul' or 'self'. In time *atman* came to mean the 'Soul' or 'Self' of the universe.

Avatar: an incarnation of deity, particularly in reference to Rama and Krishna as *avatars* of Vishnu.

Bhakti: devotion or love, particularly in relation to Krishna

Bhakti yoga: yoga of devotion to a personal god. It involves meditation on sacred images, chanting, invocation and service of the god.

Brahman: creator of the world, ultimate Reality.

Cakras: biospiritual 'centres' of psychic energy that lie along the central *nadi* or 'channel' which runs up through the centre of the spine.

Darshan: 'sight' of or audience with a devotee's god or guru.

Hatha yoga: physical and other exercises designed to give perfect mastery of the body with a view to changing it into a divine body.

Ishvara: 'god' as understood in the yogic philosophy of Patanjali

Japa: devout 'recitation' of one of God's names or of a mantra. *Japa* can be done aloud or in silence, spoken or sung.

Jnana yoga: from *jnana* meaning 'wisdom' or 'transcendent knowledge'. *Jnana yoga* involves a special kind of liberating, intuitive knowledge or wisdom which cannot be acquired by study or research in the intellectual sense. It aims at attaining to the state of *advaita*.

Kaivalya: 'aloneness' or 'isolation': the goal of Patanjali's yoga.

Karma: 'action' and its consequences which work themselves out either in one's present life or in a subsequent incarnation.

Karma yoga: 'yoga of action'. Action must be carried out with a sense of detachment from the fruit of that action. The good works with detachment are believed to burn off one's (bad) *karma*.

Kriya yoga: a variant of *hatha yoga*, specialising in *kriyas* or cleansing rituals for nasal passages, stomach, intestines and so on.

Kundalini: from *kundala* meaning 'ring' or 'coil'. It refers to the energy that is believed to lie dormant at the base of the spine in every human being. In yogic literature *kundalini* (alternately *shakti*) is conceived of sometimes as a goddess, at other times as a coiled serpent.

Kundalini yoga: techniques to activate the potential *kundalini* energy and induce it to ascend through the *sushumna*, passing in turn through each *cakra*. The objective is to bring about the 'marriage' of *shakti* and *shiva* in the *sahasrara cakra*.

Mantra yoga: use of mantra, either chanted or silently. It is frequently associated with one of the other forms.

Maya: the 'illusion' that anything can be truly real outside and independently of *brahman*.

Nada: inner 'sound' which can be located in the right ear during meditation. Focusing on this point can give rise to the experience of sounds such as those produced by the ocean, a waterfall, a kettledrum, a bell or a flute.

Nadi: a 'channel' of *prana* or life-force throughout the body.

Purusha: 'spirit' or 'soul', the true nature of the individual according to Patanjali.

Prakriti: 'Nature', the material principle in Patanjali's philosophy.

Prana: 'breath', 'wind', 'vitality' or 'life-force'; commonly associated with the breath.

Pranayama: the 'control' of *prana* by means of breathing exercises.

Raja yoga: 'royal' yoga. It involves getting one's mind to slow down and become still and thus to disengage from the material world.

Saccidananda or *Sat-cit-ananda*: 'being, knowledge, bliss' in reference to God; the Trinity conceived in Indian terms.

Sahasrara: refers to the 'lotus with a thousand petals', the highest *cakra* at the crown of the head.

Samadhi: 'ecstasy', 'contemplation'; it refers to the higher stages of meditation characterised by an experience of *advaita* or oneness.

Samsara: the cycle of birth, death and rebirth; reincarnating after death into another physical body in order to suffer or work off one's *karma* as determined by previous lives.

Sankirtana: 'group chanting' of mantras.

Sannyasa: 'renunciation' of the world in order to seriously pursue a yogic or spiritual path.

Sannyasi: one who has embraced the state of *sannyasa*.

Sanskara: an unconscious impression left by actions in the present or previous lives. *Sanskaras* influence the way a person will think, judge and act in the future.

Shakti: identical with *kundalini* when this is conceived in a personalised form as goddess; counterpart and consort to *shiva*.

Shaktipat: initiation by a touch or a look of the guru, leading to the awakening of *kundalini*.

Shiva: god of destruction, pure Being-Consciousness, consort of *shakti*.

Siddha: a perfect master who has attained enlightenment and is fully Self-realised; one who possesses *siddhis*.

Siddhi: 'power', especially in the context of magic

Tantra: a text contain tantric instruction; more generally the tradition behind *tantric yoga*.

Tantric yoga: a system of yogic techniques aimed at incarnating spirituality within the body and in everyday realities. Some tantrists employ the ritual of 'the five M's' – *madya* (wine), *matsya* (fish), mamsa (meat), *mudra* (parched grain) and *maithuna* (sexual intercourse). There are so-called 'right-hand' schools which understand and use these elements in a metaphorical sense, and 'left-hand' schools which use them literally.

Upanishad: literally 'session'; the *upanishads* are a series of mysticophilosophical texts dating from the eighth to the fourth centuries BC.

Veda: India's earliest religious texts, dating between 1800 and 1000 BC.

Vedanta: 'Veda's end', the religious philosophy of the *upanishads*.

Vishnu: conserving, protecting god, whose principal avatars are Rama and Krishna.

Yoga: 'union' with God or the universal Soul (*atman*); practices or techniques designed to bring about such a union.

NOTES

HISTORY OF YOGA

1. Georg Feuerstein, *Yoga – The Technology of Ecstasy* [Los Angeles, 1989], p. 111. This work has been an important source for the material in this chapter.
2. *Bhagavad-Gita*, VI.31 as found in Feuerstein, *op. cit.*, p. 162.
3. *Cf.* Marcia Eliade, *Yoga – Immortality and Freedom* [Princeton, 1970], pp. 54–55, 96–97.
4. Psychologist John H. Clark as quoted in Feuerstein, *op. cit.*, p. 194.
5. Eliade, *op. cit.*, p. 93.
6. That this form of yoga is still current is evidenced in a BBC documentary a few years ago on the life of a present-day *aghori in which all of these features appeared. See also Bal Krishna Shukla, 'Hinduism and Occultism: Opponents or Allies?' in *Spirituality in East and West* [Aarhus], No. 3 (1996), pp. 14–15, which contains a description of current nocturnal activities by *aghoris on the burning ghats at Varanasi.
7. See chapter on Kundalini yoga, p. 75.
8. See chapter on Bhakti yoga p. 43.
9. For a detailed account of tantric initiation and the five M's, see Agehananda Bharati, *The Tantric Tradition* [London, 1965], chapters 7 and 9.

WHAT IS YOGA

1. As found in Feuerstein, *op. cit.*, p. 152.
2. Yogasutras I, 2 as translated by Fernando Tola and Carmen Dragonetti in *The Yogasutras of Patanjali* [Delhi, 1987], p. 3.
3. *Cf.* Feuerstein, *op. cit.*, p. 204.
4. The information in this paragraph is mainly from Eliade, *op. cit.*, pp. 146–161. The passage quoted is from p. 150.
5. All of this paragraph from Theodore Benfey, *Sanskrit-English Dictionary* [reprint, New Delhi, 1982], entries 'YUJ' on p. 744 and 'yoga' on p. 749.
6. 'According to Patanjali, Yoga does not mean union but spiritual effort to attain perfection through the control of the body, senses and mind, and through right discrimination between *Purusha* and *Prakrti.*' Chandradhar Sharma, *A Critical Survey of Indian Philosophy*, p. 169; '[Yoga is] those physical and mental processes which are used to discover man's inner essence, which is the Supreme'; Arthur Avalon, *The Serpent Power*, p. 181. Yoga 'is the process by which the identity of the individual soul and the Supreme Soul is realised by the Yogis'; Sri Swami Sivananda, *Science of Yoga*, Volume Four [Rishikesh, UP, 1982], p. 151.
7. Eliade, *op. cit.*, pp. 216–217 for the quotations and information in this paragraph.

YOGA IN SOME NEW AGE AND NEW RELGIOUS MOVEMENTS

1. For this section *cf.* Robert S. Elwood (Ed.), *Eastern Spirituality in America* [New York, 1987], pp. 16–19; 215.

2. The information on Ramakrishna and Vivekananda in this paragraph is based on Anders Blichfeldt, 'Tantra in the Ramakrishna Math and Mission' in *Update* [Aarhus], VI, 2 (June, 1982), pp. 30–47.

3. Simeon Stylites, 'Hindu Fundamentalists on the Move' in the journal *Areopagus* [Hong Kong], III, 4 (Trinity, 1990), p. 21.

4. Johannes Aagaard, 'Hinduism's World Mission' in *Update* [Aarhus], VI, 3 (September, 1982), pp. 5–7. In this article Dr Aagaard describes his fortuitous discovery of all the back issues of *Hindu Vishva*, which supplied crucial evidence for the existence of a concerted missionary effort on the part of India's guru movements.

5. From a report 'Hinduism on the Move' in *Areopagus* [Hong Kong], V, 1 (Advent 1991), p. 38.

6. For the archaeological and historical repudiation of the VHP's claims re Ayodhya see Brian K. Smith, 'Re-envisioning Hinduism and Evaluating the Hindutva Movement' in *Religion* [Lancaster], vol. 26, No. 2 (April 1996), pp. 123–124.

7. James G. Lochtefeld, 'New Wine, Old Skins: the Sangh Parivar and the Transformation of Hinduism' in *Religion* [Lancaster], vol. 26, No. 2 (April 1996), p. 112.

8. *Cf.* Lochtefeld, *op. cit.*, pp. 109–111.

9. Steven Hassan *Combatting Cult Mind Control* [Rochester, Vt, 1988] and Flo Conway and Jim Siegelman, *Snapping – America's Epidemic of Sudden Personality Change* [New York, 1978] are among of the better representatives of anti-cult literature. See also Conway and Siegelman, 'Information Disease' in *Science Digest*, (January 1982), pp. 86–92; A. Deikman, M. D., *The Wrong Way Home – uncovering the patterns of cult behaviour in American society* [Beacon Press, Boston 1990].

TONY QUINN'S POPULAR YOGA

1. The quotations in the paragraph are from *Blueprint for Living*, No. 19 [August 1989], pp. 1, 5.

2. *Blueprint*, No. 24 [Spring, 1991], pp. 2, 4.

3. *Ibid.*, No. 19, p. 5 for the last two quotations.

4. Both of these quotes from *Blueprint*, No. 18 [April 1989], p. 1.

5. *Ibid.*, No. 24, p. 4.

6. *Ibid.*, No. 19, p. 5.

7. *Ibid.*, No. 18, p. 1.

8. *Ibid.*, No. 19, p. 5.

9. *Ibid.*, No. 16 [September, 1988], p. 3.

10. *Ibid.*, No. 28 [Autumn, 1992], p. 14.

11. *Ibid.*, No. 34 [Autumn, 1994], p. 7.

12. *Ibid,* No. 36 [Summer, 1995], p. 4.

13. *Ibid.*, p. 5.

14. All quotations in this paragraph are from *Blueprint,* No. 35 [New Year, 1995], p. 11.

15. *Ibid.*, No. 19, p. 5. The bracketed phrase in italics is mine.

16. *Ibid.*, No 17, p. 2.

17. See *Blueprint,* No. 36 (Summer 1995), p. 6.

18. Mark 11.22–25, The quotation is from the *Good News Bible* [London, 1976].

19. Henry Wansbrough, OSB in *A New Catholic Commentary on Holy Scripture,* [Fuller, Johnston, Kearns eds., London, 1969], p. 973.

20. *Cf. Blueprint,* No. 19, p. 5.

21. Quotes in this paragraph are from Ernest Wood, *Yoga* [Harmondsworth, England, 1959], pp. 59, 61.

22. *Blueprint,* No. 16, p. 3.

23. Tom McArthur, *Understanding Yoga – A Thematic Companion to Yoga and Indian Philosophy* [Wellingborough, 1986], p. 44.

24. *Blueprint,* No. 16, p. 3.

25. *Ibid.*, p. 1.

26. See for example, Feuerstein, *op. cit.*, pp. 118, 150, 250.

CLASSICAL HATHA YOGAS

1. *From Calendar 1992 – Sivananda Ashram Yoga Ranch,* Woodbourne NY.

2. For much of the above information on Swami Sivananda and his ashram, *cf.* Vishal Mangalwadi, *The World of Gurus* [Second Edition, New Delhi, 1987], pp. 63–67.

3. As found in *Hindu Scriptures,* translated by R. C. Zaehnar [London, 1966], pp. 37.

4. For the background to the rise of modern guru movements see *The World of Gurus,* pp. 5 –26.5.

5. Sri Swami Sivananda, *Science of Yoga,* IV [Rishikesh, 1982], p. 166.

6. Gordon Melton, *Encyclopedia of American Religions* [4th ed., 1993], p. 933.

7. *Cf.* Swami Satyananda Saraswati, *Yoga Nidra* [Munger, Bihar, fifth edition 1984] for a detailed explanation of *yoga nidra.* Guided imagery exercises are found on pp. 110–113, 120–123.

8. From a pamphlet entitled *A Cordial Invitation* [Munger, 1994] published by the Bihar School inviting followers of Satyananda to be present for the ending of his period of silence. This pamphlet is the source of the information in this paragraph.

9. *Himalayan Institute Quarterly* [Honesdale, PA] Fall 1988, p. 4. See also Melton, *op. cit.*, p. 917.

10. *Himalayan Institute Quarterly, loc. cit.*
11. From *Yoga* [London, 1989], a pamphlet of the Iyengar Yoga Teachers' Association.
12. B. K. S. Iyengar, *Light on Yoga* [London, 1976], p. 520.
13. From the sixth chapter of the *Bhagavad Gita* as quoted by Iyengar in *Light on Yoga*, pp. 19, 22.
14. *Light on Yoga*, p. 46. The quotation echoes Luke 13: 24.
15. *Ibid.*, pp. 39, 49. This 're-visioning' of Patanjali is not followed through by all of Iyengar's disciples, e.g., Silva, Mira and Shyam Mehta in *Yoga – The Iyengar Way* [London, 1990], pp. 164–170.

BHAKTI YOGA AND THE HARE KRISHNAS

1. Chandradhar Sharma, *A Critical Survey of Indian Philosophy* [New Delhi, 1960], pp. 380–381.
2. J. Isamu Yamamota, *Hare Krishna, Hare Krishna* [Downers Grove, Illinois, 1980], p. 9.
3. The information in this section is culled from Satsvarupa Dasa Goswami, *Prabhupada – He Built a House in Which the Whole World Can Live* [Los Angeles, 1983]; Melton, *op. cit.*, p. 920.
4. His Divine Grace A. C. Bhaktivedanta Swami Prabhupada, *The Science of Self-Realisation* [London, 1977], p. 26.
5. *Ibid*, pp. 29–30.
6. His Divine Grace A. C. Bhaktivedanta Swami Prabhupada, *Introduction to Bhagavad-gita* [Borehamwood, Herts., 1992], p. 50. See also *The Science of Self-Realisation*, pp. 129, 131; also *The Perfection of Yoga* [London, 1972], p. 52.
7. The translation of this verse of the Gita is by Prabhupada and is taken from *The Perfection of Yoga*, p. 61.
8. Sharma, *op. cit.*, p. 380. See also on this point Geoffrey Parrinder, *Avatar and Incarnation* [New York, 1982], p. 84.
9. Both quotations in this paragraph are from the sixteenth century *Sri Chaitanya Charitamrita* as found in Parrinder, *op. cit.*, p. 84.
10. His Divine Grace A. C. Bhaktivedanta Swami Prabhupada, *Bhagavad-gita As It Is* [New York, 1972], p. xi.
11. *The Science of Self-Realisation*, p. 150.
12. Of interest here is a verse from the tenth-century *Bhagavata Purana XI.14.24*: 'He whose speech is interrupted by sobs, whose heart melts, who unashamedly sometimes laments or laughs, or sings aloud and dances – (such a person) endowed with devotion to Me purifies the world'. This text is found in Feuerstein, *op. cit.*, p. 218.
13. *The Science of Self-Realisation*, pp. 146–148; 162.
14. *Ibid.*, pp. 139–145; 192–193; 270–274.
15. *The Perfection of Yoga*, p. 21.

16. Quoted in Robert Elwood (ed.), *Eastern Spirituality in America* [New York, 1987], pp. 30–31 .

17. *Encyclopaedia Britannica* (fifteenth edition, Chicago 1975), Vol. 16, p. 124.

18. Bede Griffiths, 'Mantra' in *New Catholic Encyclopaedia*, IX, p. 174.

19. Patanjali, *Yogasutras*, I, 28 as found in Ernest Wood, *Yoga* [London, 1959], p. 189: 'There should be repetition of (the mantra AUM), *with concentrated thought upon its meaning*'. (italics mine).

20. *The Science of Self-Realisation*, p. 101.

21. *Ibid.*, p. 147.

22. *Ibid.* Similar physiological effects such as to these have been observed within the *bhakti yoga* tradition as far back as the eleventh century. See Surendranath Dasgupta, *A History of Indian Philosophy* [Cambridge, 1949], III, p. 28.

23. Parrinder, *op. cit.*, p. 83.

24. Parrinder, *op. cit.*, p. 83.

25. Dasgupta, *op. cit.*, III, 389–390.

26. Flo Conway and Jim Siegelman, *op. cit.*, p. 181.

27. 'Information Disease' in *Science Digest* [January, 1982] pp. 86–92.

28. John Hubner and Lindsey Gruson, *Monkey on a Stick – Murder, Madness and the Hare Krishnas* [Orlando, Florida, 1980], p. 180.

29. Hubner and Gruson, *op. cit.*, p. 382; Melton, *op. cit.*, p. 921.

30. Hubner and Gruson, *op. cit.*, p. 394; Melton *op. cit.*, p. 922.

31. Hansadutta has his own website on the Internet, found at http://www/geocities.com/Tokyo/1148/about/html.

32. For this paragraph see Melton, *op. cit.*, pp. 915, 937, 938.

33. Hubner and Gruson, *op. cit.*, p. 135.

MANTRA YOGA AND TM

1. The main source for the information on the School of Economic Science are Peter Hounam and Andrew Hogg's highly critical study entitled *Secret Cult* [Tring, Herts., UK, 1985]; William Shaw, *Spying in Guruland* [London, 1994], pp. 119–142.

2. Anthony O'Brien (TM teacher) in 'Transcendental Meditation and Christian Belief' in *Doctine and Life* [Dublin], vol. 30, No. 2 (February, 1979), p. 104.

3. For the information in this section *cf.* Melton, *op. cit.*, pp. 945–946; Eileen Barker, *New Religious Movements – A Practical Introduction* [3rd ed., London,1992], pp. 213 – 214; Massimo Introvigne, *Le Nuove Religioni* [Milano, 1989], pp. 314 –315.

4. *Cf.* R. K. Wallace and Herbert Benson, 'The Physiology of Meditation' in *Scientific American* [San Francisco], 226 (February 1972), pp. 84-90.

5. Herbert Benson, MD with Miriam Z. Klipper, *The Relaxation Response* [London, 1977], p. 113.

6. *Ibid.*, pp. 70 – 71.
7. From a pamphlet entitled 'Transcendental Meditation of Maharishi Mahesh Yogi', published by the London branch of the TM organisation, p. 1.
8. Mark Hosenball, 'Master class goes sour on the old guru' in the *Sunday Times* [London], 2 December, 1986.
9. Leon S. Otis, 'Adverse Effects of Transcendental Meditation' in *Update* [Aarhus], ix, 1 (March, 1985), p. 42.
10. Maharishi Mahesh Yogi, *The Science of Being and Art of Living* [SRM, 1963], p. 19. I encountered this quotation in Una Kroll, *TM – A Signpost for the World* [London, 1974], p. 38
11. From 'Transcendental Meditation of Maharishi Mahesh Yogi', p. 2.
12. M. Hiriyanna, *Outlines of India Philosophy* [London, 1932], p. 71.
13. *Ibid.*, p. 72.
14. The quotations in this paragraph are from a full-page advertisement in *Time* magazine, 26 December 1983, p. 46.
15. From a resolution of the Illinois House of Representatives dated 24 May 1972, quoted from a TM sponsored pamphlet entitled 'Scientific Research into Transcendental Meditation' [London, 1972].
16. For quotations in this paragraph see *Ibid.*, pp. 4, 6.
17. See report by Peter Maarbjerg in *Update* [Aarhus], ii, 1 (April, 1978), p. 27; *The World of Gurus*, pp. 137–138.
18. Steve Richards, *Levitation – What it is, How it works, How to do it* [Wellingborough, UK, 1980), p. 65; the rendering of the mantras in English and also the correspondence with the meditators' ages, is slightly different in 'Vital Information on Transcendental Meditation' published on the Internet by the Dialogue Centre International [Aarhus, Denmark], http://www.dci.dk/elephant/tm.html#mantra, downloaded on 20 January 1997.
19. For an explanation of how Sanskrit seed mantras should be pronounced see Ernest Wood, *Yoga* [revised ed., Harmondsworth, UK, 1962], pp. 151–152 with fn. 1 on page 151.
20. Swami Vishnu Devananda, *Meditation and Mantras* [New York, 1981], p. 81.
21. *Ibid.*, p. 76 for the quotations in this paragraph.
22. Bharati, *op. cit.*, pp. 245, 251, 264: 'he feeds her betel-nut in a betel-leaf *(tambula)*, touches her pudenda for an instant, and mutters the syllable *aim* one hundred times'.
23. Eliade, *op. cit.*, p. 212.
24. *Ibid.*, p. 215.
25. As found in *The World of Gurus*, p. 138
26. See *The World of Gurus*, p. 139. The words quoted are actually from the Ethical Committee of the Danish Medical Society.
27. Bharati, *op. cit.*, p. 187.
28. *Ibid.*, pp. 186–187.

29. *Ibid.*, pp. 93, 189, 245.

30. *Ibid.*, pp. 185–186, 189.

31. For information in this section *cf.* Mark Albrecht and others, 'A Spiritual Tour of India' in *Update* [Aarhus], pp. v, 1 (May 1981), pp. 3–8. On some difficulties encountered in the development at Noida see Anuradha Dutt, 'The Troubled Guru' in *The Illustrated Weekly of India* [Bombay], pp. cix, 3 (17 January 1988), pp. 8–17.

32. For these figures see 'The Rise and Decline of Transcendental Meditation' [with Daniel H. Jackson] in Rodney Stark and William Sims Bainbridge, *The Future of Religion – Secularisation, Revival and Cult Formation* [Berkeley, 1985], pp. 284–303.

33. *Cf.* John Burns, Party Leader, The Natural Law Party (Ireland) in a letter to *The Examiner* [Cork], 10 December, 1996.

34. R. Stark and W. S. Bainbridge, *op. cit.*, p. 302.

35. Feuerstein, *op. cit.*, pp. 165.

36. R. Stark and W. S. Bainbridge, *op. cit.*, p. 303.

Yoga of Sound and Light

1. *Cf.* Julian Johnson, *The Path of the Masters* [Beas, Punjab, 13th rev. ed. 1985], p. xl.

2. For the material in this paragraph see 'A Spiritual Tour of India', compiled by Mark Albrecht in *Update* [Aarhus, Denmark] V, [May 1981], p. 19; Vishal Mangalwadi, 'Five Paths to Salvation in Contemporary Guruism', *Update*, IX, 4 [December 1985], pp. 27–29.

3. Johnson, *op. cit.*, Preface by Pierre Schmidt, p. xxxii.

4. *Ibid.*, p. 103.

5. *Ibid.*, pp. 102, 142.

6. *Ibid.*, p. 95.

7. *Ibid.*, p. 99.

8. *Ibid.*, p. xxxix.

9. *Ibid.*, pp. 143, 156, 401.

10. *Ibid.*, p. 149.

11. *Ibid.*, pp. 227 – 228.

12. *Ibid.*, p. 411.

13. *Ibid.*, p. 414.

14. *Ibid.*, p. 417.

15. See 'Update' in *Areopagus* (Hong Kong), II, 2 (Epiphany, 1989), p. 50.

16. See 'Update' in *Areopagus* (Hong Kong), III, 2 (Epiphany, 1990), p. 50.

17. *Cf.* David Christopher Lane, 'The Making of a Spiritual Movement: The Untold Story of Paul Twitchell and Eckankar' (independent study, Department of Religious Studies, California State University, Northridge 1978), p. 19. For this reference and information generally on Twitchell and Eckankar

see *SCP Journal* (Berkeley, 1979), *Eckankar – A Hard Look at a New Religion*.

18. Johnson, *op. cit.*, p. 221.
19. *SCP Journal*, pp. 14–15.
20. *Cf.* Eileen Barker, *New Religious Movements* [London, 1992], p. 175.
21. *The Eck Mata Journal*, [Menlo Park], X [1985], pp. 5, 6, 9, 11–12, 14, 16; *The Mystic World* (Eckankar Newsletter), Fall 1985, p. 5.
22. See *SCP Journal*, pp. 45–47.
23. Sources for the 'four techniques' include Ronald Enroth, *Youth, Brain-washing and the Extremist Cults* (Grand Rapids, 1977) pp. 137–138 and Mangalwadi, 'Five Paths' in *Update*, IX (December, 1985), pp. 28–29.

KUNDALINI YOGA AND SWAMI MUKTANANDA

1. A classical study of the structured practice of *kundalini* yoga is to be found in Arthur Avalon, *The Serpent Power – The Secrets of Tantric and Shaktic Yoga* [Dover ed., New York, 1974], pp. 181–256.
2. From a programme published by the Oakland Siddha Yoga Ashram, February–April, 1992.
3. For data on Muktananda's early years *cf.* Mangalwadi, *The World of Gurus*, pp. 200–202.
4. Swami Muktananda, *Chitshakti Vilas – The Play of Consciousness* [revised ed., Ganeshpuri, 1982], p. 75. The initiation is described on pages pp. 72–76.
5. *Ibid.*, pp. 85–86.
6. *Ibid.*, p. 87.
7. *Ibid.*, p. 102.
8. *Ibid.*, pp. 108–111.
9. *Ibid.*, pp. 113–115.
10. *Ibid.*, pp. 155 and 180–186, a chapter entitled 'The World of Sounds'. In this chapter *nada* is identified with God (p. 182).
11. *Ibid.*, pp. 133, 165.
12. *Ibid.*, p. 143. See also pp. 157, 159 and 164.
13. *Ibid.*, pp. 202–205.
14. *Ibid.*, p. 190.
15. *Ibid.*, p. xxxiii.
16. *Cf.* Feuerstein, *op. cit.*, pp. 281–286; Eliade, *op. cit.*, pp. 301–307.
17. Feuerstein notes one example on pp. 213–214. *Chitshakti Vilas*, pp. 303–325, records the testimony of five disciples (one of them Gurumayi) who received *shaktipat* from Muktananda and subsequently experienced *kundalini* phenomeona such as visions, inner sounds, 'floating', burning sensations and automatic execution of yoga postures.
18. Quoted from Oakland Siddha Yoga Ashram [programme], February–April 1992.
19. Feuerstein, *op. cit.*, p. 239.

20. *Ibid.,* p. 237.
21. *The Advisor,* IV, 5 (October/November 1982), p. 16.
22. On the scandals within the Siddha Yoga movement see Melton, *op. cit.,* pp. 935–936; Russell Chandler, *Understanding the New Age* [UK ed., Milton Keynes, 1989], 64 and Mangalwadi, *The World of Gurus,* pp. 209–211.
23. These quotations from Muktananda's writings are found in Mangalwadi, *The World of Gurus,* pp. 205–206.
24. *Chitashakti Vilas,* pp. 131, 143, 145 respectively.
25. Mangalwadi, *The World of Gurus,* p. 209.

THE POLITICAL YOGA OF ANANDA MARG

1. This according to a report in *Update* [Aarhus], October 1980.
2. *Cf.* Aghehananda Bharati, *The Ochre Robe* [Second Ed., Santa Barbara, 1980], pp. 47–54.
3. Prabhat Ranjan Sarkar, *Proutist Economics – Discourses on Economic Liberation* [Calcutta, 1992], p. 78.
4. According to a report headed 'Villagers oppose Hindu sect's plan for child centre' in the London *Times,* 30 September 1996.
5. Gheorghe Samoila, 'AMURT Romania – Raising Potential Ananda Marga Missionaries for Activities Abroad?' in *Spirituality East and West* [Aarhus], No. 2, 1996, pp. 8–10. Reports.
6. Prabhat Ranjan Sarkar, *op cit.,* pp. 15–16
7. *Ibid.,* p. 130.
8. *Ibid.,* pp. 21, 29.
9. *Ibid.,* p. 79. *Cf.* Prabhat Ranjan Sarkar, *Idea and Ideology* [Calcutta, 1959], p. 71.
10. '... the sacred duty of the *sadvipras* shall be to protect the righteous and the exploited and subdue the wicked and the exploiters through the application of force'; from *The Principles of Prout* in *Proutist Economics.* The Principles date from 1961. The same point is made in many of Sarkar's statements; e.g.: '*Sadvipras* ... may have to resort even to physical violence, because the *sadvipras* will have to strike at the source of the power [of the class] which is tending to become the exploiter', *Idea and Ideology,* pp. 73–74.
11. From an Ananda Marg booklet entitled *16 Points For Self Development – A Summary of Ananda Marga Spiritual Practices* [1976], pp. 45–46.
12. *Cf. The Tantric Tradition,* p. 87.
13. Fritjof Capra, *The Tao of Physics* [Fontana, Suffolk, 1976], p. 256.
14. Raimundo Panikkar, *The Vedic Experience – Mantramanjari* [London, 1977], p. 892.
15. T. O. Ling, 'Shiva/Shaiva' in *The Penguin Dictionary of Religions* [Harmondsworth, Middlesex, 1984], pp. 299–300.
16. Partha S. Banerjee in 'Cult of Terror – inside Ananda Marg' in *The Onlooker*

[Bombay, 22 November 1983], p. 18.

17. S. N. M. Abdi, in 'The Margis', *The Illustrated Weekly of India*, 27 October 1985, p. 15.

18. Banerjee, *The Onlooker*, pp. 15, 17.

19. From *16 Points For Self Development*, p. 29.

20. From the Indian magazine *Mahima*, July–August 1978

21. Acharya Paritoshananda Avadhuta and Acharya Vishwarupananda Avadhuta, eds., *The Awakening of Self – A Practical Approach to Tantra* [Calcutta, 1988], p. 1.

22. *Ibid.*, p. 98.

23. *16 Points For Self Development*, p. 37.

24. Of interest here is a comment by David Gold in 'Explaining Hindu Communalism' in *Religion* [London], 21 (October, 1991), p. 367: '... contemporary communal politicians seem to have mastered in the public arena, abilities long sought in the magical world by yogis intent on harnessing the psychic energies around them'.

RAJA YOGA AND THE BRAHMA KUMARIS

1. The above national details were a few of many reported in a newsletter issued by the organisers of MMOP entitled *Minute by Minute*, pp. iii, 1–3.

2. *When We Change* ..., a pamphlet published by the BKWSU, p. 8.

3. The information in the next section was found mainly in *When We Change* ...; Barker, p. 169; Melton, *op. cit.*, pp. 909–910; Introvigne, *op. cit.*, pp. 318–319.

4. Frank Gaynor, *Dictionary of Mysticism* [London, 1974], p. 92.

5. See the testimony of one ex-member in Shaw, *op. cit.*, pp. 93–94.

6. This term was used by Brahma Kumari meditation teacher Mike George at a Stress Management Seminar in Dublin, 15 June 1995.

7. *Ibid.*

8. These phrases are selected from *Practical Meditation* [3rd ed., London, 1993], pp. 3, 7, 31.

9. Mike George at the Seminar referred to above.

10. *Practical Meditation*, pp. 9, 20.

11. *Ibid.*, p. 5.

12. *Ibid.*, p. 31.

13. *Ibid.*, p. 21.

14. *Ibid.* pp. 8–9, 17–19.

15. Taken from Eliade, *Yoga*, p. 91. The author of *Practical Meditation* rightly states (p. 14) that the term *sanskara* has 'no simple translation'. Alternatives to the text might be 'subliminal impression', 'subconscious residues'.

16. *Practical Meditation*, p. 14.

17. *Ibid.*, p.18.

18. *Ibid.*, p. 21.

19. Mircea Eliade, *Patanjali and Yoga* [New York, 1975], p. 25.
20. Surendranath Dasgupta, *Yoga as Philosophy and Religion* [London, 1924], p. 13.
21. Eliade in *Patanjali and Yoga* [New York, 1975], p. 44, puts the word 'enslaved' in parentheses to underline the deeper truth that 'The self is pure, eternal, free; it would be impossible to subjugate it because it would be incapable of maintaining relations with anything other than itself. But man believes that the purusha is enslaved ...'
22. Patanjali's *Yogasutras*, I, 2, as translated by Tola and Dragonetti, *op. cit.*, p. 3. Eliade gives an alternative translation of Patanjali's *cittavrttinirodhah* as 'the abolition of states of consciousness' in *Patanjali and Yoga*, p. 51 and 'the suppression of states of consciousness' in *Yoga, Immortality and Freedom*, p. 36.
23. *Yogasutras*, I, 3 as found in Tola and Dragonetti, *op. cit.*, p. 7.
24. *Cf.* Tola and Dragonetti, *op. cit.*, pp. 61–63, 181–185.
25. Dasgupta, *op. cit.*, pp. 159–161
26. *Cf. Ibid.*, pp. 87–89.
27. Eliade, *Yoga*, pp. 74–76 and *Patanjali and Yoga*, pp. 88–90.
28. Eliade, *Yoga*, p. 93.
29. Eliade, *Patanjali and Yoga*, p. 46.
30. *Raja Yoga*, a leaflet of the B. K. Raja Yoga Centre, San Francisco, p. 2.
31. *Practical Meditation*, p. 31.
32. *Raja Yoga*, p. 3.
33. *Practical Meditation*, p. 31.

CAN YOGA BE CHRISTIAN?

1. See for example M. Basilea Schlink, *Christians and Yoga?* [Darmstadt-Eberstadt, 1975] and a flyer entitled 'Surely there's no harm in yoga – or is there?' published by the Diasozo Trust [Sandwich, Kent, 1980]. This latter carries an illustration of a figure in lotus posture engulfed in flames.
2. Published by Inter-Varsity Press, Leicester, 1983. Other Christian scholars whose standpoints have much in common with that of Allan include Vishal Mangalwadi, Moti Lal Pandit and Bal Krishna Shukla; all authors of articles published by Dialog Center International, based at Aarhus in Denmark. Profressor Johannes Aagaard, President of the Dialog Center is the outstanding European representative of this thinking.
3. *Op. cit.*, p. 32.
4. 'Letter to the Bishops of the Catholic Church on some aspects of Christian Meditation' issued by the Congregation for the Doctrine of the Faith on 15 October, 1989, signed by Joseph Cardinal Ratzinger, Prefect and Bishop Alberto Bovone, Secretary. The document is divided into short sections, the numbers of which are indicated in the following footnotes of the present work.

5. *Ibid.*, section 23.
6. *Ibid.*, sections 9, 27, 28.
7. *Ibid.*, section 28.
8. *Ibid.*, section 16.
9. *Ibid.*, section 28.

JEAN DÉCHANET AND HATHA YOGA

1. The sources for this biographical sketch are J.-M. Déchanet, *Christian Yoga* [Tunbridge Wells, 1960], pp. 2–3, 6–9, 104–106 and most of all a letter kindly written to me by P. Christian Papeians de Morchoven, archivist of Déchanet's monastery, Saint-Andriesabdij, Bruges.
2. *Christian Yoga*, p. 1.
3. E.g., Ignatius of Antioch, Irenaeus, Origen and Gregory of Nyssa. *Cf.* G. W. H. Lampe, *A Patristic Greek Lexicon* [Oxford, 1961], pp. 1097 and 1546 under the headings of *pneuma* and *psyche* respectively.
4. Jean Déchanet in 'Notes Doctrinales' in *Guillaume de Saint-Thierry: Lettre aux Freres di Mont-Dieu* [Paris, 1975], pp. 399–400. Bede Griffiths also understood the last of the 'three': *spiritus* to be the realm of grace. (This from his Hibbert Lecture broadcast by BBC Radio 4 on 21 September 1989).
5. *Cf.* 'William of Saint-Thierry' by B. Lohr in *New Catholic Encyclopedia* [Washington, 1967], Vol XIV, pp. 938–939.
6. Déchanet in 'Notes Doctrinales', p. 401.
7. *Christian Yoga*, p. 2.
8. Abhishiktananda, *Prayer* [London, revised ed., 1972], p. 74. Bede Griffiths, on the other hand, did use the term 'Christian Yoga'. See *Return to the Centre* [London 1976], pp. 137–138.
9. *Christian Yoga*, pp. 3 – 4.
10. *Ibid.*, p. 45. See also p. 31.
11. *Ibid.*, p. 15.
12. Quotations in this paragraph are from *Christian Yoga*, pp. 54, 56 and 57 respectively.
13. *Ibid.*, pp. 83.
14. *Ibid.*, pp. 85.
15. *Ibid.*, pp. 32, 104–107.
16. *Cf. Christian Yoga*, pp. 121–122.
17. *Ibid*, p. 125.
18. Quotations in this paragraph are from pp. 145–147 of *Christian Yoga*.
19. *Ibid.*, p. 156.
20. *Ibid.*, *Cf.* pp. 131 and 143–144.
21. *Ibid.*, pp. 39–40, 110, 112.
22. *Ibid.*, pp. 14.

1. *Christian Meditation – The Gethsemani Talks*, John Main [Benedictine Priory of Montreal, Second Edition 1982], p. 3.
2. *Ibid.*
3. John Main, *Word into Silence* [London, 1980], p. vi.
4. This fact was communicated to the author by Laurence Freeman and Paul Harris (Christian meditation teacher) at Gort Mhuire Conference Centre, Dublin, August 1990.
5. *The Spiritual Teaching of Ramana Maharshi*, Joe & Guinevere Miller eds. [Berkeley & London, 1972], pp. 11, 62.
6. *Ibid.*, p. 49.
7. *Ibid.*, p. 70.
8. *Ibid.*, p. 8.
9. *Ibid.*, p. 66.
10. *Ibid.*, p. 60–61.
11. *Ibid.*, p. 18.
12. From a letter to Rosie Lovat, quoted in *In the Stillness Dancing – The Journey of John Main*, Neil McKenty [London, 1986], p. 123.
13. For the material of this paragraph see for example chapters 12 and 13 of McKenty, *op. cit.*, pp. 132–166.
14. *The Spiritual Teaching of Ramana Maharshi*, p. 50.
15. *Cf.* McKenty, *op. cit.*, p. 133
16. Gerry Pierse, CSSR, 'Preparing for Meditation: From The Exercises to the Mantra', *Religious Life Review* [Dublin], xxviii (July–August 1989), p. 179.
17. Examples are John 14.17; 15.5; Romans 8.10–11; Galatians 2.19 – 20.
18. Laurence Freeman, 'All are Called to Contemplation' in *Religious Life Review*, xxviii (March–April 1989), p. 65.
19. 'Memories of John Main' in *Religious Life Review*, xxvii (March–April 1988), p. 71.
20. *Ibid.*, p. 73.
21. Laurence Freeman, OSB, *Light Within* [London, 1986], p. 4.
22. John Grennan, ODC, 'The Call to Contemplation', *Religious Life Review*, xxviii (March/ April 1989), p. 79.
23. John Grennan, ODC, 'Discerning Contemplative Prayer' in *Religious Life Review*, xxvii, 130, January–February 1988, p. 12.
24. Laurence Freeman, 'All are Called to Contemplation' in *Religious Life Review*, xxviii (March–April 1989), p. 64.
25. Gerry Pierse, CSSR, 'Preparing for Meditation: From The Exercises to the Mantra', *Religious Life Review*, xxviii (July–August 1989) pp. 177–181.
26. Gerry Pierse, CSSR, 'The Grennan-Freeman Exchange' *R.L.R.* xxviii (May–June 1989) pp. 154–156.

ANTHONY DE MELLO'S SADHANA

1. *Contact with God – Retreat Conferences* [Anand, India, 1990].
2. *Ibid.*, pp. 173–180.
3. See for example *Wellsprings* (Anand, 1984), pp. 129–134.
4. As pointers to how De Mello was influenced by the Rogerian school see for example Carlos Valles, *Mastering Sadhana* [London, 1988], pp. 123, 125.
5. John O. Stevens, *Awareness: exploring, experimenting, experiencing* [Moab, Utah, 1971].
6. The quotation and the information in this sentence is from Eleanor O'Leary, *Gestalt Therapy – Theory, Practice and Research* [London, 1992], p. 13.
7. *Cf.* De Mello's book *Sadhana – a Way to God* (Anand, 1978), p. 63.
8. *Cf.* for example Stevens, *op. cit.*, pp. 22, 34 and *Sadhana*, pp. 12, 55.
9. Stevens, *op. cit.*, pp. 33–34 and *Sadhana*, pp. 12–13.
10. Stevens, *op. cit.*, pp. 3 –52.
11. The De Mello version can be found for example in John Callanan, SJ, *The Spirit of Tony de Mello* [Cork, 1993], p. 89.
12. *Sadhana*, pp. 81 – 82 and *Awareness*, pp. 152 – 153.
13. *Sadhana*, p. 25.
14. *Sadhana*, p. 17
15. *Sadhana*, pp. 52–53
16. *Ibid.*, p. 10.
17. *Ibid.*, p. 15, 56.
18. *Ibid.*, p. 24.
19. *Ibid.*, p. 26.
20. *Ibid.*, pp. 50–51.
21. 'The Mirage' and 'The River' in *Wellsprings*, pp. 158–163.
22. *Ibid.*, p. 160.
23. *Ibid.*, pp. 190ff and *Sadhana*, p. 79
24. pp. 91–92. The exercise in *Wellsprings* called 'The Symphony' (pp. 176–182) is a more extended and developed form of 'Fantasy on the corpse'.
25. *Sadhana*, Exercises 25 to 28 inclusive, pp. 83–91. These exercises are taken up in a modified form in *Wellsprings*, in the exercises beginning on pp. 149, 153, 167, 171, 183 in the section entitled 'Life'.
26. *Ibid.*, pp. 15–17, 209–212.
27. *Ibid*, pp. 27–29 and 41–43 respectively.
28. *Ibid.*, pp. 162, 164–166.
29. *Ibid.*, pp. 66, 82.
30. *Ibid.*, pp. 197–199.
31. *Ibid.*, pp. 140–144.
32. *Sadhana*, p. 95.
33. *Ibid.*, pp. 76–77.
34. *Ibid.*, pp. xv–xvi.

35. De Mello's understanding of the different levels of meaning hidden in stories is to be found in a whole tradition of storytelling that spans the religious/secular divide. See for example William J. Bausch, *Storytelling – Imagination and Faith* [Mystic, Ct., 1984], p. 172: 'religious tales (people) do tell. How can we tell? Because so often they tell stories, however unconsciously, that deal with life's meaning, life's fundamentals, life's mysteries. Even when they do not realise it, people are posing ultimate questions in their storytelling.' *Cf.* also pp. 25, 38, 58 and 109 of this book.

36. Specifically *Song of the Bird* (1982), *One Minute Wisdom* (1985), *One Minute Nonsense* (1987) and *Prayer of the Frog* [Volume I] (1988) all from the Gujarat Sahitya Prakash, Anand, India.

37. *Prayer of the Frog*, p. xxi.

38. Valles, *op. cit.*, p. 113.

39. Valles, *op. cit.*, pp. 54–55.

40. *Sadhana*, pp. 35–36 and *Wellsprings*, pp. 281–283.

41. Feuerstein, *op. cit.*, p. 191.

42. *Sadhana*, pp. 42 – 44. *Cf.* Feuerstein, *op. cit.*, p. 234.

43. *Sadhana*, p. 32. 'The Ocean' in *Wellsprings*, pp. 253–254 is very similar.

44. *Sadhana*, p. 41 and a corresponding exercise 'The Caress' in *Wellsprings*, pp. 251–252.

45. *Sadhana*, pp. 37–41

46. Feuerstein, *op. cit.*, p. 252

47. Valles, *op. cit.*, p. 148

48. For this quotation from Theophan the Recluse I am indebted to E. F. Schumacher, *A Guide for the Perplexed* [Abacus edition, London, 1978], pp. 86–88.

49. *Contact with God – Retreat Conferences*, p. 85.

50. *Sadhana*, p. 110.

51. *Ibid.*, pp. 108–109. See also *Contact with God*, p. 90.

52. Parmananda Divarkar, SJ, in the Foreword to *Prayer of the Frog*, p. xviii.

ABHISHIKTANANDA AND JNANA YOGA

1. Most of the information in this section has been derived from James Stuart, *Swami Abhishiktananda – His life told through his letters* [New Delhi, 1989]. The concluding quotation is found on p. 339 of this work.

2. Stuart, *op. cit.*, p. 360.

3. Stuart, *op. cit.*, p. 37.

4. *Cf.* for example, Wayne Teasdale, *Towards a Christian Vedanta* [Bangalore, 1987], p. 95.

5. Abhishiktananda, *Prayer* [London, revised ed., 1972], p. 4. See also his letter to Sister Sara Grant in Stuart, *op. cit.*, p. 289.

6. Abhishiktananda, *The Further Shore*, [New Delhi, 1984], p. 100.

7. *Ibid.*, p. 99.
8. Stuart, *op. cit.*, p. 317.
9. *Prayer*, p. 39.
10. *The Further Shore*, p. 106.
11. *Ibid.*, p. 64.
12. Ramana as quoted by R. Balasubramanian, 'Two Contemporary Exemplars of the Hindu Tradition: Ramana Maharshi and Shri Candrashekharendra Sarasvati' in *Hindu Spirituality – Vedas through Vedanta* [New York/London, 1989], p. 372.
13. *Ibid.* See also Joe and Guinevere Miller, eds., *The Spiritual Teaching of Ramana Maharshi* [Berkeley and London, 1972], p. 6; also *The Further Shore*, p. 111.
14. As found in Heinrich Zimmer, *Philosophies of India*, Joseph Campbell ed. [Princeton, NJ, 1969], p. 462–463.
15. *Ibid.*, p. 463.
16. *Prayer*, p. 40.
17. *Ibid*, p. 74.
18. *Ibid.*, p. 40.
19. *Ibid.*, p. 42.
20. *Ibid.*, p. 76.
21. *Dasgupta*, I, pp. 418, 422, and elsewhere; Hiriyanna, pp. 54, 59, 63; A. L. Basham, *The Wonder that was India* [Fontana, Calcutta, 1967], p. 331. In Zimmer, *Philosophies of India*, the index on p. 665 lists 'Monism (non-dualism)' with a large number of entries, thus by clear implication equating monism and *advaita*. S. Radhakrishnan in *Indian Philosophy* [London, 1931], I, p. 37 in speaking of 'some of the Upanishads' as well as Shankar and others uses the expressions 'pure monism' and 'extreme monism'.
22. *Oxford Dictionary of the Christian Church*, [Oxford, 1983], p. 931.
23. St Elmo Nauman Jr, *Dictionary of Asian Philosophies* [Secaucus, New Jersey, 1978], p. 2.
24. Raimundo Panikkar, *The Vedic Experience – Mantramanjari* [London, 1977], p. 867.
25. *The Further Shore*, pp. 66–67.
26. *Ibid.*, p. 67.
27. *Ibid.*, p. 67.
28. Stuart, *op. cit.*, p. 319; *cf.* also *The Further Shore*, pp. 115, 134.
29. *The Further Shore*, pp. 108–109.
30. Dasgupta, *op. cit*, p. 436.
31. Zimmer, *op. cit.*, p. 427.
32. *The Further Shore*, p. 115.
33. From 'Gnosis' by Pheme Perkins in *Dictionary of Fundamental Theology* [English ed., New York, 1994], p. 341.
34. Zimmer, *op. cit.*, p. 412. See also pp. 410, 413.

35. Stuart, *op. cit.*, p. 323.

BEDE GRIFFITHS AND SHANTIVANAM

1. The earlier part of Bede Griffiths' life is described in his book *The Golden String* [London, 1954].
2. Muz Murray, *Seeking the Master* [Neville and Spearman, 1982], p. 5.
3. Bede Griffiths, *The Marriage of East and West*, [London, 1982], pp. 174–177.
4. *Ibid.*, p. 190.
5. *Ibid*, p. 88.
6. Bede Griffiths, *Return to the Centre*, pp. 23–24. Bede refers the reader to the *Summa Theologiae*, I, XV, I, ad 3, which reads: '... Deus secundum essentiam suam est similitudo omnium rerum. Unde idea in Deo nihil est aliud quam Dei essentia.' The point that Aquinas makes in this entire article is that the likeness or form of everything that is made must first exist in the mind of the Maker. But within God this prototypical form can be nothing other than the divine essence itself existing from eternity, since God is an undivided Unity, not made up of or containing different parts.
7. Griffiths, *op. cit.*, p. 24.
8. *Cf.* for example, H. Bergson, *Creative Evolution* [London, 1911], p. 46: 'each individual may be said to remain united with the totality of living beings by invisible bonds'; A. N. Whitehead, *Science and the Modern World* [Cambridge, Mass, 1923], p. 151: 'no individual subject can have independent reality'; A. Carrel, *Man the Unknown* [London, 1935], p. 266: 'the independence of each individual from the others and from the cosmos is an illusion'; P. Teilhard de Chardin, *The Phenomenon of Man* [London, 1965], p. 48: 'The farther and more deeply we penetrate into matter, by means of increasing powerful methods, the more we are confounded by the interdependence of its parts.'
9. 'Quantum theory ... has come to see the universe as an interconnected web of physical and mental relations whose parts are only defined through their connection to the whole', Fritjof Capra, *The Tao of Physics* [London, 1976], p. 147.
10. Bede Griffiths, 'Emerging Consciousness for a New Humankind: Emerging Consciousness and the Mystical Traditions of Asia'– a lecture quoted in Teasdale, pp. 51–52.
11. *In Return to the Centre*, 31 fn, Bede refers to the *Summa Theologiae*, I–II, 81, 1 when he says: 'All men, as Aquinas says, are one Man'. The text of Aquinas reads: 'omnes homines qui nascuntur ex Adam, possunt considerari ut unus homo, inquantum conveniunt in natura, quam a primo parente accipiunt'. The context is the doctrine of original sin and its transmission which is explained in terms of a fundamental unity of the human species. Another significant text of Aquinas is *In III Physicorum*, xi, p. 385: 'Definitur enim

unumquodque totum esse "cui nihil deest" sicut dicimus hominem totum aut arcam totam, quibus nihil deest eorum quae debent habere. Et sicut hoc dicimus in aliquo singulari toto, ut est hoc particulare vel illud, ita haec ratio competit in eo quod est vere et proprie totum, scilicet in universo, extra quod simpliciter nihil est.' The point made here is that the universe alone is truly and properly whole, because there is nothing outside of itself for it to lack. See also *Summa Theologiae*, I, pp. 65, 2; II–II, pp. 65, 1 and elsewhere.

12. *Return to the Centre*, 30. The same quotation and argument is found in *Christ in India* [Bangalore, 1986], p. 34. This work, a collection of lectures by Bede, was originally published in 1966 under the title *Christian Ashram*.

13. *Return to the Centre*, pp. 30–32.

14. Bede Griffiths, *The Cosmic Revelation: The Hindu Way to God* [Springfield, Ill., 1983], p. 118.

15. Geoffrey Moorhouse, *Om – An Indian Pilgrimage* [London, 1993], p. 139.

16. *The Marriage of East and West*, pp. 175–176.

17. *Ibid.*, p. 177 for the phrases quoted in this paragraph.

18. *Ibid.*, p. 177.

19. *Ibid.*, p. 179.

20. Advaita and Trinity [Big Sur], cassette, side 1. This reference is found in Teasdale, *op. cit.*, p. 112. Drawing particularly on tape recordings of Bede's talks, as well as his written works, Teasdale gives a detailed analysis of Bede's thinking on *advaita*, Saccidananda, the Trinity, interpersonal relationship and *maya*, see pp. 103–131.

21. Teasdale, *op. cit.*, pp. 117, 129.

22. *Ibid.*, p. 178.

23. *Return to the Centre*, p. 142.

24. *Return to the Centre*, pp. 137–138. See also *Christ in India*, p. 24.

25. *Return to the Centre*, p. 142.

26. Bede Griffiths, 'In Jesus' name' in *The Tablet* [London], 18–25 April 1992, p. 498.

27. From a cassette by Bede, quote by Teasdale in *op. cit.*, p. 147.

28. Thomas Matus, *Yoga and the Jesus Prayer Tradition* [Ramsey, NJ, 1984].

29. *Ibid.*, p. 89.

30. *Return to the Centre*, p. 138. This work of Bede's was, of course, published a number of years before Matus' book.

31. *The Marriage of East and West*, pp. 165–166.

32. *Ibid*, p. 191.

33. *Christ in India*, p. 168.

YOGA IN CHRISTIAN ASHRAMS

1. Frank Gaynor (Ed.), *Dictionary of Mysticism* [London, 1974], p. 17.

2. Vandana, *Gurus, Ashrams and Christians* [London, 1978], p. 19.

3. Fr D. S. Amalorpavadass, 'Main Categories of Hindu Philosophy and Spirituality' in *Indian Christian Spirituality* [Bangalore, 1982], p. 159.

4. Muz Murray, *Seeking the Master* [Neville and Spearman, 1982], p. 5.

5. For clarification on this point of the ashram tradition I am indebted to Sister Vandana (private correspondence).

6. Michael O'Toole, 'Help Western Youth in India' in *Update* [Aarhus], vii, 3 (September 1983), pp. 61–62; Svend Boysen, 'First Steps: Meeting Western Youth in India' in *Areopagus* [Hong Kong], I, 1 & 2 (Fall, 1987), pp. 8–11; DCI Volunteers, 'Goa's Praise to Jesus' Ashram' in *Areopagus*, i, 3 & 4 (Spring–Summer, 1988), pp. 13–14.

7. Michael O'Toole, *Christian Ashram Communities in India* [Indore, 1983], p. xv.

8. Fr Amalor's biodata is taken from an obituary written by Fr Paul Puthanangady, current Director of the NBCLC, in *The Examiner* [Bombay], 9 June 1990.

9. 'The NBCLC Campus a Living Synthesis of Indian Christian Theology and Spirituality' in *Indian Christian Spirituality*, p. 239.

10. *Anjali Ashram*, [a pamphlet issued by the ashram and written by Amalor], p. 18.

11. *Ibid.*, p. 14; see also Amalor's 'Main Categories of Hindu Philosophy and Spirituality' in *Indian Christian Spirituality*, p. 151.

12. Matus, *op. cit.*, p. 39.

13. 'The Chapel "Saccidananda", Unique Place of God-Experience' in *Indian Christian Spirituality*, p. 256c.

14. *Ibid.*, p. 249.

15. *Gurus, Ashrams and Christians*, p. 75.

16. From a retreat talk given by Vandana in Navan, Ireland, 27–30 October 1995.

17. All of this paragraph is based on Sister Vandana's *Nama Japa* [Bombay, 1884], pp. 1–78. This book – already translated into German and Hindi – is dedicated to Swami Krishnananda, one of the senior-most gurus of Sivananda Ashram, Rishikesh. Its foreword was written by Swami Chidananda.

18. 'Concluding Reflections and Questions' in Vandana Mataji [Ed.], *Christian Ashrams – A Movement with a Future?* [Delhi, 1993], p. 69.

19. The material for this paragraph particularly and for much of the entire section is based on conversation and correspondence with Sister Vandana.

MORE INTERESTING BOOKS

BODY-MIND MEDITATION
A GATEWAY TO SPIRITUALITY

LOUIS HUGHES, OP

You can take this book as your guide for a fascinating journey that need not take you beyond your own hall door. For it is an inward journey, and it will take you no further than God who, for those who want him as a friend, lives within. On the way to God-awareness, you will be invited to experience deep relaxation of body and mind.

Body-Mind Meditation can help you become a more integrated balanced person. It is an especially helpful approach to meditation if the pace of life is too fast for you, or if you find yourself frequently tense or exhausted.

PETER CALVEY
THE MYSTIC

DAVID TORKINGTON

A master of the Christian spiritual life, David Torkington presents the last of his Peter Calvey books. Through the lives of his parents, Peter likens the various stages of the spiritual search for God to a successful marriage. The marital analogy is central to the whole work, showing clearly how the mystic way is for all. The work places mysticism back at the heart of the Christian life and gives readers a wealth of practical help and encouragement to support them on their spiritual odyssey.

PETER CALVEY
THE HERMIT

DAVID TORKINGTON

This a fast-flowing and fascinating story of a young priest in search of holiness and of the hermit who helps him. The principles of Christian Spirituality are pin-pointed with a ruthless accuracy that challenges the integrity of the reader, and dares him to abandon himself to the only One who can radically make him new. The author not only shows how prayer is the principal means of doing this, but he details a 'Blue Print' for prayer for the beginner, and outlines and explains the most ancient Christian prayer tradition, while maintaining the same compelling style throughout.

Over 35,000 of this bestseller have been sold.

PETER CALVEY
THE PROPHET

DAVID TORKINGTON

This book is first and foremost a brilliant exposition of the inner meaning of prayer and of the profound truths that underlie the spiritual life. Here at last is a voice that speaks with authority and consummate clarity amidst so much contemporary confusion, of the only One who makes all things new and of how to receive Him.

The Spirit of
Tony De Mello
A Handbook of Meditation Exercises

John Callanan, SJ

This book captures the essence and spirit of Tony de Mello. He was a great teacher. Some said he was a dangerous one. He constantly challenged himself, the world within which he lived and those he came into contact with. For some this element of challenge was both unsettling and confusing. Tony said that our security does not lie in thoughts or ideas no matter how profound. Neither does it lie in traditions – no mattered how hallowed. Security can only reside in an attitude of mind and a readiness to reflect deeply, thus subjecting any and every belief to rigorous questioning.

So Tony urged people to question, question question. Questions often make us uncomfortable. They do, however, force us to reflect and thus ensure our growth.

John Callanan has started the book with an opening chapter on the basics of prayer. Then he moves on to try and give a flavour of the ideas and themes which gave so much zest and life to Tony de Mello's presentations. The exercises in this book are based on the prayer-style which Tony himself developed during his retreats.

Spiritual and Thought-Provoking Quotations

Des MacHale

In the crazy, rushed world of today this wonderful collection of quotations from the great philosophers, poets and thinkers provide an opportunity to stop and reflect.

Do you know who said:
Forgiveness is the scent the violet leaves on the heel that crushes it.

To a man with an empty stomach, food is God.

I try. I fail. I try again. I fail better.

Alcoholism isn't a spectator sport. Sooner or later, the whole family gets to play.

Man is born broken. He lives by mending. The grace of God is glue.

No snowflake in the avalanche ever feels responsible.

Most children suffer from too much mother and too little father.

The best kind of sex education is a loving family.

To sing is to pray twice.

Nothing lasts forever – not even your troubles.

SOMETHING UNDERSTOOD
A SPIRITUAL ANTHOLOGY

EDITED BY SEÁN DUNNE

This anthology contains a rich selection of writing on many aspects of spirituality. They include God, pain, prayer, love, loss, joy and silence. Drawing on the great traditions of Christian Spirituality, Seán Dunne has assembled pieces by dozens of writers, among them Thomas Merton, Simone Weil, Teresa of Avila, John Henry Newman, and Dietrich Bonhoeffer. He has also chosen from the work of creative writers such as Patrick Kavanagh, John McGahern, Kate O'Brien and George Herbert. With a wide selection of material that ranges from just a few lines to many pages *Something Understood* is a perfect source for reflection on aspects of spirituality that have been the concern of men and women through the centuries.